j362.4 B496p
Berger, Gilda.
Physical disabilities
$6.90

NOV 1 3 1979   CHEROKEE

Memphis and Shelby
County Public Library and
Information Center

For the Residents
of
Memphis and Shelby County

PHYSICAL DISABILITIES

BY GILDA BERGER

PHYSICAL DISABILITIES

FRANKLIN WATTS | NEW YORK | LONDON | 1979

Photographs courtesy of: The President's Committee on Employment of the Handicapped: pp. 4, 30, 93; United Cerebral Palsy Associations, Inc.: p. 8; New York Public Library Picture Collection: p. 19; National Institute of Neurological and Communicative Disorders and Stroke, Linda Bartlett, photographer: p. 48; Cutter Laboratories: p. 74; National Easter Seal Society for Crippled Children and Adults, Inc.: p. 110

Art courtesy of Vantage Art, Inc.

Library of Congress Cataloging in Publication Data
Berger, Gilda.
    Physical disabilities.

    Includes bibliographies and index.
    SUMMARY: Discusses a variety of physical disabilities, societal attitudes towards them, and legislation dealing with the problems of the disabled.
    1. Physically handicapped — Juvenile literature. [1. Physically handicapped] I. Title.
HV30.B44   362.4   78-10106
ISBN 0-531-02927-1

Copyright © 1979 by Gilda Berger
All rights reserved
Printed in the United States of America
6 5 4 3 2 1

CONTENTS

1 "DISABLED NOT ALLOWED" 1

2 WHO ARE THE PHYSICALLY DISABLED? 6

3 THE DISABLED THROUGH HISTORY 14

4 PROBLEMS OF THE DISABLED 24

5 NERVE AND MUSCLE DISORDERS: 33
  Cerebral Palsy
  Epilepsy

6 OTHER NERVE AND MUSCLE DISORDERS: 45
  Multiple Sclerosis
  Muscular Dystrophy
  Spina Bifida
  Polio

7 BONE AND JOINT DISORDERS: 60
  Amputations
  Scoliosis
  Arthritis

8   CHRONIC HEALTH PROBLEMS: 68
    Hemophilia
    Heart Disease
    Diabetes
    Cystic Fibrosis
    Asthma
    Anemia

9   SENSORY IMPAIRMENTS: 86
    Blindness
    Deafness
    Multiple Handicaps

10 A NEW DAY   108

    BIBLIOGRAPHY   113

    FURTHER READING   114

    INDEX   116

PHYSICAL DISABILITIES

1

"DISABLED NOT ALLOWED"

The young woman and her friend got at the end of the long line outside the movie theater. The picture they wanted to see, "Coming Home," is a popular film about a wounded Vietnam War veteran, who is wheelchair-bound.

The long line inched forward. Finally the couple reached the box office. But the ticket-seller refused to sell the young woman a ticket. "Move aside, please," she said. "N-e-x-t."

When she refused to move, the manager was called. He was quite blunt. "Look, I'd like to sell you a ticket," he explained, "but I can't because you're in a wheelchair. There is no way someone in a wheelchair can see a movie here. The theater itself is up a flight of steps. Sorry, but you'll just have to leave."

"But I *want* to see the movie," she replied. "My friend will help me up the steps. I'm in a wheelchair, it's true. But this is a movie about someone in a wheelchair."

The manager thought for a moment. "Listen, lady," he insisted, "it won't work. The theater is crowded. There is no room for the wheelchair. I can't change the way things are. This building is just not built for handicapped people."

Still, she refused to leave. There were some in line who just wanted the line to keep moving. Others spoke up for the young woman.

Grudgingly, the manager gave in at last. Through tears of pain and anger the woman paid the admission price and took her ticket. Her friend helped her up the stairs. She watched the film while seated in her wheelchair from a spot that the manager found for her behind the last row of seats.

Do you know that millions of people in this

country are not allowed to enter theaters, stores, museums, libraries, shopping centers, restaurants, parks, playgrounds, and schools because they cannot climb steps or pass through narrow doorways or gates? That they are not allowed to live in many buildings, or work in many offices or factories, or attend many schools or colleges? That they may not board many trains, buses, or planes?

Do you know that people who are deaf cannot work in factories with machines that signal danger by a ringing bell? That people who are blind cannot use a telephone unless it has raised letters and numbers on the dial?

Do you know that many of the disabled cannot use public restrooms because the toilet stalls are too small for a wheelchair? or the door pushes in instead of swinging out? or the sinks do not have enough room underneath for a wheelchair? or the water faucets are set too far back?

None of these places have signs saying, "Disabled Not Allowed." But they might just as well. Steps and high curbs, narrow doors and halls, poorly designed rooms, furniture, and fixtures keep out the disabled as effectively as barbed wire fences.

But it is not physical barriers alone that keep many disabled persons from leading full and useful lives. Psychological barriers can sometimes cause even more pain and frustration. Ignorance, fear, prejudice, intolerance, and discrimination are often more restricting. Lack of understanding and sympathy thwarts those with disabilities.

Persons with disabilities are stared at, whispered about, even laughed at. People shout at them, talk down to them, or — what is even worse — ignore

them. Well-meaning parents and teachers sometimes overprotect them. Thoughtless people feel sorry for them, and show them pity.

The disabled are becoming increasingly angry at being shut out of so many places, and being made to feel so unworthy and incapable. They want to lead full, rich lives — to go to school, become financially independent, develop social relationships, and participate in the life of their communities to the fullest extent possible.

Much progress has been made in recent years to eliminate many of the physical and psychological barriers against the disabled. But as the young woman at the movie theater found out, much more remains to be done.

This barrier-free hall allows the disabled to live more normal social lives.

2 WHO ARE THE PHYSICALLY DISABLED?

The physically disabled are people who have defects or disorders which prevent them from doing things that others of their age can do. They may lack the ability to control parts of their body. They may be missing a limb. They may have complete or partial loss of vision or of hearing. Their heart, lungs, muscles, bones, or nervous system may be diseased, damaged, or deformed. They may have an incurable illness.

Perhaps you have a friend, a relative, a classmate, or a neighbor who is physically disabled. Maybe you yourself have a physical disability. Someone said, "All of us are physically limited. It is just a matter of degree."

The physically disabled person is sometimes called physically impaired or physically handicapped. Although the words are often used interchangeably, they do have slightly different meanings.

Physically *impaired* people have physical defects — the loss of a limb, a nerve or bone disorder, a chronic health problem. The impairment makes them physically *disabled* — they are unable to walk, cannot see, cannot hear. The extent to which they are prevented from leading a "normal" life — attend school, get a job, drive, take part in sports, get married, have children — is the extent to which they are physically *handicapped*.

In this book the physically disabled are all people who have activity limitations because of physical impairments. Only the leading permanently disabling conditions are included. These conditions may or may not be physically handicapping.

Many infants are born with disabling defects. It might be a growth problem, so that the child never reaches full size. It might be a body deformity due to muscular dystrophy, or a lack of muscle control due

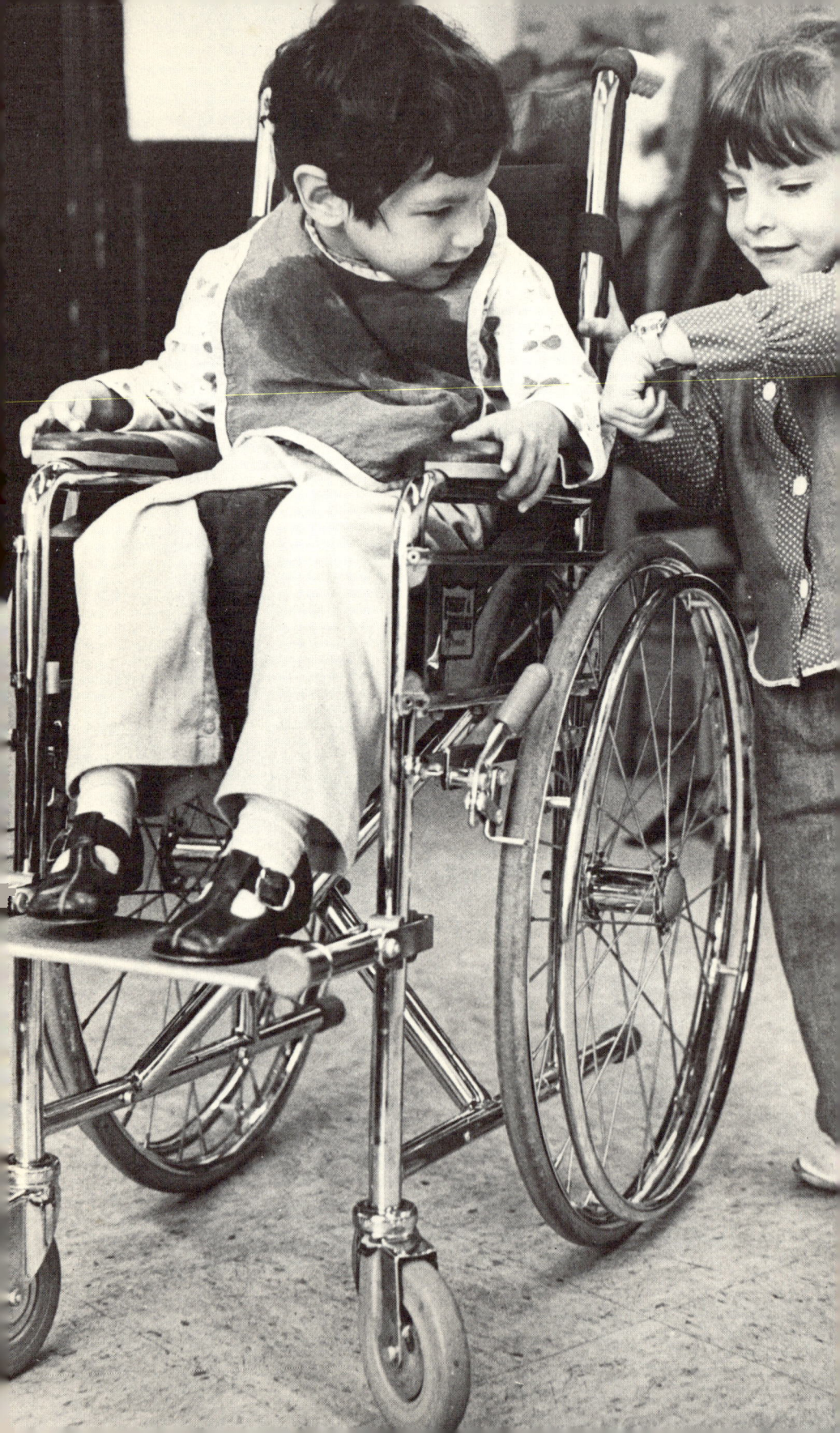

to cerebral palsy. Or it might be that the baby is born without sight or hearing, with a defective heart, or with a damaged arm or leg.

Others become disabled as a result of disease. Deformed joints are the result of arthritis. A limit to the amount of activity possible is part of heart disease and diabetes. A serious infection in the eyes or ears may lead to visual or hearing impairments. Paralysis follows some diseases of the nervous system or of the muscles.

Still others are disabled in accidents. Permanent injuries, severe disabilities, and disfigurements can result from serious auto collisions, or accidents at work, at home, in the street, or from fires.

No one is sure exactly how many persons in the United States are physically disabled. The most recent and reliable source is the 1970 survey of the National Center for Health Statistics. They estimate that there are nearly thirty million physically disabled in this country; just about one out of every seven men, women, and children.

The total figure is broken down this way: three million can only walk with the help of crutches, canes, or braces; 500,000 require wheelchairs. Eleven million are hearing impaired; 2½ million are deaf. Over eight million are visually impaired; 1½ million are blind. And nearly two million are homebound because of various chronic diseases and disorders. (Other estimates vary, depending on which impairments are included and how the statistics were assembled.)

The millions of people who are physically dis-

**This boy was born
with cerebral palsy.**

abled include a cross-section of the population. They are young and old, rich and poor, black and white, Christian and Jew, male and female. They live in every city, town, and village of every country in the world.

Among them are persons with mild disabilities as well as severe disabilities. There are people who manage very well and those who can do little for themselves. In this number are those with determination and will power who achieve more than seems possible and those who do little because they are afraid to try. There are many who grow up to be independent and self-sufficient and others who live empty and hopeless existences.

There is a long, ever-growing list of disabled men and women who have achieved fame and success. They show that having an impairment and being disabled does not mean being handicapped and dependent.

Franklin Delano Roosevelt was stricken with polio at the age of thirty-nine, and was left partially paralyzed. Yet he was elected the thirty-second president of the United States by many people who were not even aware that he could not walk without canes and braces.

Ludwig van Beethoven, one of the greatest composers of all time, lost his hearing at the age of thirty. During the remaining years of his life, though, he wrote some of his best-known works.

The ancient Greek poet Homer was blind, as was John Milton, the 17th-century English poet, when he composed some of his most famous epic poems.

The German writer Heinrich Heine had a spinal disease that left him paralyzed and half blind. Yet he continued to compose poetry and prose in bed until his death in 1856 at the age of fifty-nine.

Charles Steinmetz, one of the most brilliant inventors in the field of electricity in the early years of this century, was only four feet tall and had a deformed, misshapen body.

Louis Pasteur did some of his most important work, including the discovery of a cure for rabies, after his left leg and arm were completely paralyzed.

Helen Keller, though blind and deaf from the age of two, learned to write and to speak. She inspired many by her courage and enthusiasm.

The outstanding violinist, Itzhak Perlman, paralyzed since he fell ill with polio at the age of four, walks with crutches. He concertizes throughout the world while seated on the stage.

The well-known track star Glenn Cunningham set several track records in the Olympics, even though doctors said he would never walk again after he was severely burned in a fire.

Wilma Rudolph limped and had to wear a high shoe due to nerve damage which she suffered as a child. Still, she became the star woman athlete from America in the 1960 Olympics.

Alexander de Seversky lost a leg in an air battle during World War I, but went on to become the leading aircraft designer of his time.

Pianist Paul Wittgenstein presented concerts of music for the left hand alone for more than forty years, because his right hand had to be amputated early in his career.

The physically disabled are also ordinary people who refuse to allow their disabilities to interfere with their dreams and hopes.

Murray B. had polio as a child. He learned to write and to feed himself, using only his feet. He travels freely now, and even deposits the money in the coin box with his feet when he boards a bus.

As a young woman of seventeen, Justine C. lost

the use of both arms and legs in a diving accident. Though she is paralyzed, she feeds herself, brushes her own teeth, and washes herself. Not only does she look after herself, but she also manages her own business.

Florence B. was born with a defective heart. Yet she became a successful and highly respected psychotherapist.

Gerald P., born without legs, drives his own automobile and supports his family of eight by running a travel agency.

Doctors amputated Larry M.'s left arm when he was only twelve. He continues to play football, hockey, and even baseball.

Christine R. earns an excellent living as a cocktail pianist in a fine restaurant, even though she was born blind and has had to learn all the music by memory or from recordings.

Lorraine S., who is deaf, runs a large center to train workers who are deaf and blind.

The numbers of physically disabled in our society have been going up in recent years. The main reason is that people are living longer now than they did in the past. Advances in medicine and sanitation have extended the life expectancy for most individuals.

Since more older people are disabled than young people, the percentage of disabled continues to grow. The fact is that between the ages of forty-five and sixty-four about 25 percent of the people are disabled. Past the age of sixty-five over 60 percent are disabled.

Each year, as doctors learn more, persons with life-threatening illnesses or injuries are returned to health. In many cases, though, the person is left with some permanent disability. For example, at the end of World War I, only about 5 out of every 1,000 diers who were paralyzed in both legs survived for twenty years. Since the end of World War II in 1945, about 800 out of every 1,000 paralyzed soldiers have survived.

The number of physical disabilities due to automobile, traffic, and bicycle accidents is also on the upswing. The physically disabled with impairments due to accidents are starting to outnumber those who were born with defects or became disabled because of disease. Safety measures in autos bring down the number of deaths, but they sometimes increase the numbers of physically disabled.

Physical disabilities change what people can and cannot do. But disabilities themselves do not change people. Many disabled persons would like to get this idea across to the non-disabled. A young man who is paralyzed so that he cannot speak or move his arms or legs summed it up. Communicating with a pointer attached to a leather band around his head, he spelled out his message by pointing to letters printed on a tablet attached to his wheelchair: "Hey, I can do it. Maybe I do it differently than you, but I do it!"

3 THE DISABLED THROUGH HISTORY

Attitudes toward the disabled have changed through the course of human history.

Primitive people were very cruel. The survival of the tribe often depended on every member being able to hunt for food, to fight in wars, and to work around the village. Great value was placed on physical strength and speed, on keen vision and hearing. The disabled were considered a burden on the able-bodied.

Another reason for rejecting the disabled was the ancient belief that disabilities were caused by evil spirits. The disabled, some thought, were possessed by such spirits. And the only way to destroy the spirit was to kill the person.

A child born with a deformity was immediately put to death. People who developed disabilities later in life were either killed, driven out of the village, or allowed to die by neglect. One account tells of the practices in the area of Europe we now call Germany: "Old and weak parents were killed by the son. Blind, squinting, and deformed children were disposed of by the father, either by the sword, drowning, or burning. Lame and blind servants were hanged to trees."

Some of these primitive attitudes and harsh treatments carried over into the early societies of the Hebrews, Greeks, and Romans. The first Hebrews associated physical disabilities with sin. An impairment was a punishment sent by God. Although the law of Moses did not allow the killing of crippled people, the lame, the blind, and the deformed were looked on with fear and revulsion.

The Greeks believed that the physically impaired were inferior people. Since the Greeks' goal was to create a race of superior men and women, they rid themselves of those who were imperfect. In Sparta, newborn children were examined by a group of elders. The impaired were taken to a mountain gorge, where they were flung to their death.

In Athens, deformed infants were placed in special clay containers, and left to die. Later, the Romans placed defective children in baskets which were thrown into the Tiber River, or left out on a public street. It was quite common for someone to come along, take the basket home, and raise the disabled child as a slave.

During the Middle Ages, from about A.D. 400 to the late 1400s, the disabled, deformed, and those with permanent disease were thought to be possessed by the Devil. They were laughed at, cursed, stoned, and hounded from place to place. Dwarfs, hunchbacks, and others with damaged bone structures often served as jesters in the courts of the nobles. Their impairments were a source of humor, and the butt of cruel jokes. Large numbers of disabled persons, both men and women, were burned as witches. It was a carryover of the primitive idea that an impairment was the sign that an evil spirit had entered the body.

During the Renaissance, from 1450 to 1600, there were great advances in scientific thinking and understanding. Doctors began to discover some of the causes of the physical disabilities. Fewer people believed that the disabilities were caused by evil spirits, sin, or the Devil.

But John Calvin, an important church leader during the Renaissance, set back the cause of the disabled. In his Christian creed, now known as Calvinism, he stated that originally man was created perfect and pure in the image of God. Men and women who were not perfect and pure (such as the disabled) showed that they had fallen out of grace with God. The only way to be saved is through the grace of God. Good works or good deeds are of no help in achieving salvation. This view added another burden to the lives of the disabled.

The early English settlers in America looked on the disabled with compassion, but still considered them financial burdens. All those who had physical defects were prevented from coming to the New World. When someone who was already here became disabled, the British system of local public relief was applied.

One common practice in colonial times was to "farm out," or board, those who were unable to care for themselves. One Thomas Elgarr was boarded with thirty-two different families from August 1683 to December 1684.

The Revolutionary War permanently injured many soldiers and civilians as well. The young government took responsibility for their welfare. But no one tried to help them become independent. It was accepted that disabled persons were dependent, either on the government or on members of their family for support.

Even so, several people with physical defects became prominent in the early days of this country. Peter Stuyvesant wore a peg leg, since he had lost his right leg while fighting the Portuguese. He was the first governor of the Dutch colony of New Amsterdam, which is today's New York City. Stephen Hopkins signed the Declaration of Independence as the representative from Rhode Island. His hand shook as he wrote because he had cerebral palsy, a disease in which the person has great difficulty in controlling his or her muscles. And Morris May, one of the framers of the Constitution, had lost his left leg in a carriage accident. He later became Assistant Minister of Finance in the new government.

A big change in attitude toward the disabled came in the early 1800s. Many Americans and British began to regard the disabled with sympathy, and to treat them with consideration. Behind these changes was the Protestant idea that each individual must strive for perfection. The goal was to help the lame to walk, the blind to see, and the deaf to hear — using the limited medical skills that were available, as well as the power of prayer.

In 1832 in Boston, Samuel Gridley Howe organized the first school for the blind, later called the Perkins Institute. He educated Laura Bridgman, who had been left blind and deaf after an attack of scarlet fever at the age of two. He taught her to speak with her hands and to write. The girl became a celebrity, and an inspiration to many other youngsters and adults with disabilities. Many years later, Helen Keller, who also lost both her sight and her hearing before she was two years old, attended the Perkins Institute.

Thomas Hopkins Gallaudet was one of the first to help the deaf. His interest sprang from his attempts to help Alice Cogswell, a neighbor's daughter, who had become deaf at the age of four. Gallaudet taught her to be independent and self-sufficient.

Gallaudet got better results through the use of sign language than by the other method, which is to read lips. In 1817, he founded the Hartford (Connecticut) School for the Deaf. His younger son, Edward Miner Gallaudet, opened Gallaudet College, a college for the deaf, in Washington, D.C., in 1864.

People with disabilities caused by missing or damaged limbs, or deformed or diseased bodies, did not fare as well as the blind and deaf. During the 19th

Throughout history, the disabled were kept at home, rarely leaving the house.

century, they were either left to their families for all care and attention, or placed in a hospital or almshouse as charity cases.

A few were helped to overcome their disabilities. Among them was Thaddeus Stevens, a leader in Congress and a well-known fighter for the abolition of slavery. Stevens had a badly deformed foot, which caused him to bend and limp as he walked. Also, Edward Livingston Trudeau, a young doctor who found at twenty-five years of age that he had tuberculosis. Trudeau studied and researched the disease, and founded the Adirondack Cottage Sanitarium in 1884 for treatment of the disease.

The final years of the 19th century saw great industrial and urban expansion. There was also an increase in poverty and labor unrest. In the past, the factory owners had known the workers and their families personally. They felt responsible for the workers in their plants. As the factories grew in size, though, the entire system grew more impersonal. Various charitable organizations were formed to help the disabled. They provided training for youngsters with disabilities and jobs for the adults.

In the 20th century interest in workmen's compensation first arose. Workers received financial help if they were accidentally injured while working on a job. Also, the first states passed laws providing that all the handicapped must be educated. In practice, though, the handicapped were accepted into the public schools only if it did not interfere with the education of the non-handicapped.

As with previous wars, World War I, which ended in 1918, aroused public concern for wounded veterans. In 1918, Congress passed the Smith-Sears Vocational Rehabilitation Act. It gave the federal government responsibility for the education and vocational training of disabled veterans. It was the first national law specifically aimed at helping disabled people.

The shortage of workers during World War I also made Americans aware of the many men and women who were not able to work because of injuries suffered in industrial accidents. The loss of productivity as well as humanitarian concerns led to the 1920 Vocational Rehabilitation Act. This law allotted money for vocational training, counseling, and job placement, as well as for the purchase of artificial limbs for those who were hurt in job-related accidents.

During World War II, there was widespread appreciation of the heroic sacrifices of the soldiers who were returning from the battlefields with permanent disabilities. This led to an improved public attitude toward all the disabled, soldiers and civilians alike. Vocational training and rehabilitation were provided for those with disabilities so that they could work in the factories producing wartime goods, and not need charity.

Public Law 16 and the Barden-LaFollette Act of 1943 legislated vocational rehabilitation for both veterans and civilians. There was a new concern for psychological, as well as physical, rehabilitation. Contact with the community became an important goal for the disabled.

During these years, there was also a gradual shift from the large, extended family unit, to the smaller family group. Gone from the home were the grandparents and great-grandparents, the uncles, aunts and cousins who had been available in the past to help care for the disabled. As the style of living changed, more of the handicapped were placed in special institutions.

In the 1940s and 1950s organizations of parents of handicapped children, and groups of the handicapped, came into being. At first, they met only to give each other support. In time, they began to pressure federal and state lawmakers to pass new legislation to meet the specific needs of the disabled. They turned also to the courts to correct the inequalities that worked against disabled people. The results further improved the status of the handicapped.

The 1960s were a time of great social awareness. The 89th Congress reached a high point in government concern for the rights and opportunities of all Americans. Rehabilitation, especially vocational rehabilitation for the disabled, became more important. Another milestone in providing education for the handicapped was reached with the Title VI section of the 1965 Elementary and Secondary Education Act.

Even more social legislation was passed in the 1970s. The disabled, along with various racial minority groups and women, pressed their demands for equal rights. They forced society to consider their hardships.

In the field of education, some significant laws were passed during the 1970s. They climaxed in the Education of All Handicapped Children Act, Public Law 94–142, of 1975. This law is often called the Bill of Rights for the handicapped. It guarantees all handicapped youngsters the right to the most appropriate education. This education is at public expense and in the setting best suited to their needs as determined by school officials, together with the children's parents. The setting may be a regular classroom or a special classroom in a public school, a special day or residential school, or a hospital, if the child needs constant medical care.

The most important law dealing with the rehabilitation of the disabled was the Rehabilitation Act of 1973. Under its terms, all government agencies and any business, school, or other organization that receives over $2,500 in federal money must take "affirmative action" to hire and promote the handicapped. That means a positive effort must be made to seek out and employ the disabled, and to consider the disabled for promotion on the basis of their performance on the job.

The new laws of the 1970s have established the legal basis for an improved situation for the disabled. The public's growing awareness of the problems and hurdles to be overcome by the handicapped has contributed to a better social and psychological climate. And advances in medical science and technology have made many new treatments, drugs, and devices available.

4 PROBLEMS OF THE DISABLED

"When people meet us they think we don't know anything. They're uptight. They treat us like babies."

"People can't believe that a kid in a wheelchair is normal."

"People are always doing things for us, but we never have a chance to do things for ourselves or for other people."

"People look at you funny."

"People seem to be afraid of me. They stare out of curiosity. Then, when I turn around and see them staring, they get all upset."

"I wake up every day and say to myself: I'm going to have to prove myself to at least one other person today so that I can be accepted as a human being."

"Growing up disabled in America is like trying to swim the English Channel. It's a struggle all the way."

This is how some children and some adults with physical disabilities have expressed their problems. Everyone with a disability, from young to old, is aware of a whole range of difficulties in how they feel and think about themselves and how others feel and think about them.

Children who are born with a physical defect usually become aware early in life that they are "different." They soon notice the pity, the curiosity, the fear, even the rejection. The full impact of their disability, though, usually strikes when they begin to play with other children and to attend school.

In school they discover they can't run — or walk — or talk — or see — or hear — like the others. They find out that they are kept out of the play and games by unthinking youngsters. Often children who are physically disabled are unable to compete with the other children. From the very beginning, they may have to miss long stretches of school because of hospital visits.

These missed contacts with people their own age may slow down their social maturity and their development of a positive self-image. Limits to play and physical activity block the usual ways children release energy and learn about themselves and others. Often, these children feel uncertain when confronted with new situations. They fear that they will be mistreated. They are unsure of what they can do and what they cannot do. Reluctant to engage in new situations, some disabled children give up without really trying.

Of prime importance in the early years, for all children, is the attitude and behavior of the parents and other children in the family. Is the child accepted with love and understanding, or with feelings of anger and guilt? Are the parents realistic in helping the child live with his or her strengths and weaknesses? Do they either make believe that certain disabilities do not exist or exaggerate their seriousness? Do the parents help the youngster set practical goals and work to achieve them, or do they have either too low expectations or impossibly high standards? Do they fall into the trap of assuming that because the child is limited in physical abilities, he or she is also limited in mental abilities and in psychological and emotional development?

Take the case of Patty, for example. Even though the doctor said that she could walk with braces, her parents did not encourage her to leave the wheelchair. They wheel or carry her around the house. They take care of all her needs and bring her anything that she wants. They buy her clothes and more expensive gifts than they can afford.

When she is alone, Patty is often depressed, anxious, and fearful. Thoughts about her disability are never far from her mind. "Nobody likes me," she thinks to herself. "I'll probably never marry. When my parents get too old to care for me, I'll probably be put in a state hospital and spend the rest of my life there."

Paul is in a different situation. When he and his parents were given a choice between braces and wheelchair, they chose braces. They all knew it would be hard at first. Although he suffered many painful and embarrassing falls, his parents helped him learn to use the braces. They did not rush to catch him when he started to totter or fall.

Paul is treated just like his brothers and sisters. He is expected to do his share of the chores around the house. As a result, he has a good, realistic picture of the person he is. He is aware of his limitations and accepts them. He is also aware of his strong points. He has many interests and can manage most of his school activities with braces. He hopes to become a lawyer.

Parents of handicapped children, like all parents, have different ways of dealing with the stress and strain of bringing up their children. Some parents simply deny the situation. Others see it as hopeless and getting worse. Still others project anger, and withdraw from the child. This may increase their feelings of guilt. Some seldom talk about the child as an individual. They may treat him or her almost as a non-person.

Brothers and sisters of disabled children often face problems in adjustment. Siblings may experience feelings of anger, guilt, or shame toward the brother or sister in the family who others consider "strange" or "different." In one family, the last of six children was born severely afflicted with cerebral palsy. All of the family members became tense and fearful. In fact, there was so much anxiety that the youngest boy, then five years old, began to stutter.

Youngsters who grow up in families who have not accepted them have a low feeling of self-worth, a poor self-concept. They have few friends and do not get along well with others. This in turn gives rise to more negative feelings. There are those who try to hide their disability. They become shy and withdrawn. Or, they react by lashing out in anger at others.

Tim is an example of a child whose parents do not expect him to grow up. He was born with severe birth defects. Although he is ten years old, he is still wearing Pampers. He had been trained at a clinic to avoid soiling himself and he no longer needs the diapers. But he wears them because his mother is afraid of an embarrassing "accident." This keeps Tim dependent and handicapped.

Well-adjusted youngsters who function at their highest level usually come from families that grow with their children. The parents and siblings support each other. They do not completely center their lives around the child. They treat the child as "special" only with regard to the disabilities, and not as if everything about the child were different. They realize that the emotional ups and downs, the outbursts of anger, and the attempts to manipulate others are natural reactions to stress.

These parents are not afraid to seek professional help. They visit doctors and surgeons to make sure that their children are getting the best medical care. They learn about the newest devices to help the handicapped, from artificial limbs to pacemakers and motorized wheelchairs. They go to counselors for advice on educational and career planning. And they consult psychologists and meet with other parents for help in overcoming their many fears and doubts.

Adults who have physical disabilities face other problems. One big difficulty is finding work. The number of disabled who have jobs, compared to the number that could be employed, is very small. Some estimates of unemployment among the disabled say that as many as 50 percent of those able and willing to work cannot find jobs.

The problem is not only unemployment. It is also under-employment. Many of the handicapped work in sheltered workshops, which are set up to provide undemanding work for the disabled — but at very low salaries, and with little chance for advancement. Even those who work in regular jobs often earn less than the non-disabled. For example, according to the 1970 census, 12 percent of the non-disabled workers earned below the poverty level. Yet 21 percent of the disabled earned below the poverty level.

Many people say that they are for equal rights for the disabled. But in practice, all too often the disabled are treated with indifference and thoughtless acts of discrimination.

Many non-disabled persons are unwilling to enter into friendships with disabled people. They do not accept the disabled as friends, husbands, or wives. Studies show that the more severe and visible the impairment, the worse the situation. An obvious impairment has been found to be more of a barrier to friendship than difference in skin color.

One thousand people were recently asked what should be done with a blind young man and a young man crippled by a birth defect. Nearly 700 said the blind man should be put in an institution and be given a job in a sheltered workshop. Nearly 600 suggested

Without accessible parking facilities, this man would be unable to go to work.

the same thing for the physically handicapped person. Only 440 believed that they should both be given a chance to live on their own and hold down a regular job.

It is perfectly natural at first to be curious about a child or an adult with a severe disability. It is natural even to feel sympathy. The non-disabled person often feels embarrassed and ill at ease. How should I treat a person in a wheelchair? Should I offer to push? open doors? be sympathetic? How do I help a blind person? take his or her arm? offer assistance or not?

Speaking to people who have disabilities, if the situation allows, or finding out more about disabling conditions, satisfies curiosity and wipes out pity. Offer to help if you see that a disabled person needs assistance. But don't take over. Let the blind person take your arm, do not grab his or her's, if you are crossing a street together. Contact with individuals who have physical difficulties lets positive feelings and healthy attitudes grow.

Suzanne could not walk because of a birth defect that affected her muscles. But her mother decided that her daughter should share the experiences of other children her own age. At nine years of age, Suzanne was admitted to a regular elementary school.

"At first they weren't used to me, and I was nervous," said Suzanne.

The school arranged for Suzanne to have therapy to improve her speech. Her teacher adapted some of the activities in class so Suzanne could participate in nearly all of them. She also helped Suzanne to work out answers to some probing questions that she might be asked. The girl had no objections to classmates trying out her wheelchair while she was seated at her desk. She answered all of their questions as well as she could.

"After a while, things got much better," Suzanne later said. "Once kids got to know me, there was no problem at all."

Improved understanding of the problems of the disabled is leading to new attitudes, new legislation, and to greater integration of the disabled into the mainstream of life. It is becoming very clear that the most important problems of the disabled are not the disabilities themselves, but the attitudes of people toward them.

5 NERVE AND MUSCLE DISORDERS:

Cerebral Palsy
Epilepsy

Your nervous system is more complicated than the biggest and most expensive computer. It is made up of millions of tiny threadlike nerves that carry messages through the spinal cord to and from the brain. The brain and spinal cord together make up the central nervous system.

Each time you see, hear, feel, smell, or taste something, a message goes out from your sense organs. The messages are carried by the nerves in the form of tiny electrical impulses to your brain. Your brain interprets the nerve impulses and gives them meaning. You become aware that you are looking at a tree, hearing a record, lifting a heavy stone, smelling smoke, or feeling a tap on the shoulder.

Messages from the brain to various parts of your body are also carried by the nerves. The messages direct your muscles to tighten or to relax. You are able to talk, run, wiggle your fingers, sit down, or stand up. The messages also direct the muscles that are not under your conscious control to make your heart beat, your lungs take in and expel air, and your stomach to digest the food you eat.

Damage to parts of the central nervous system can cause loss of sight, of hearing, of speech, or of sensation. Nerve injuries can result in paralysis of some muscles. A destroyed nerve to a vital organ can cause death.

CEREBRAL PALSY

David is seven years old, although he is quite small for his age. He has large, bright, brown eyes with long lashes. He attends kindergarten in the local school.

Sometimes David has trouble keeping up with

the other children in the class. He does not move or control his arms and legs very well. When he finger-paints, most of the paint is on his arms and elbows. When he plays with puzzles, he has difficulty putting the small pieces into their proper places. His speech is badly slurred. It is very hard to understand what he is saying.

Yet, in some ways, David is ahead of others in kindergarten. When the teacher reads a story, he gets the meaning better than most of the others. His enjoyment of music is exceptional. David also has a remarkable memory. He knows the answers to most questions asked in class, though he finds it hard to put them into words.

David has cerebral palsy. Cerebral means it is centered in the brain; palsy means paralysis or muscle weakness. Although the disease was described in ancient times, it was not named until 1937. It is the most common birth defect and one of the most widespread crippling disorders of childhood.

Cerebral palsy is a disease that affects the muscles of the body, particularly of the arms and legs. In mild cases, the muscles may be only slightly weakened and lacking in control. In severe cases, the patient may be partially or completely paralyzed.

Except for some very rare cases, cerebral palsy is not inherited. Nor can it be caught by exposure to someone with the disease. It is caused by injury or damage to the brain, which can take place before birth, during birth, or after birth. Premature birth, with a birth weight of less than five pounds, is another frequent cause. Also, infections (such as German measles) or X-rays during the early months of pregnancy, diseases of the mother (such as diabetes), a blood incompatibility between the mother and the fetus, or a lack of oxygen to the fetus can result in cerebral palsy in the newborn.

During birth, cerebral palsy may result from an injury, particularly to the brain, or a lack of oxygen during the delivery period. About 1 out of every 200 babies born in the United States has cerebral palsy.

After birth, the more common causes of cerebral palsy are injuries to the head from falls, auto accidents, or cruel beatings by parents. Infections, hemorrhages in the brain, a lack of oxygen, or a brain tumor can also cause the disease later in life.

Cerebral palsy is a broad term that covers several different forms of the disease. The condition depends on the part of the brain that has been damaged.

In spasticity, the muscles of one or more limbs are very tight. When a person with this condition moves the limb, the muscles contract. It is almost impossible to control the length and direction of the motions. When children with spasticity try to draw a line connecting two dots, they are apt to exert too much energy. They often go out in the wrong direction, and then must change direction to reach the second dot. Most children with cerebral palsy caused by premature birth have the spastic form of the disorder.

Athetosis is a form of cerebral palsy in which the limbs move without purpose, and uncontrollably. When the person tries to move an arm or leg, its movement is usually contorted and awkward. At different times, the person with athetosis will twist and rotate the limbs, will hold the head, trunk, or limbs frozen in a distorted position for several seconds before moving, or will flail about with his or her arms, legs, or fingers. When a child with athetosis tries to

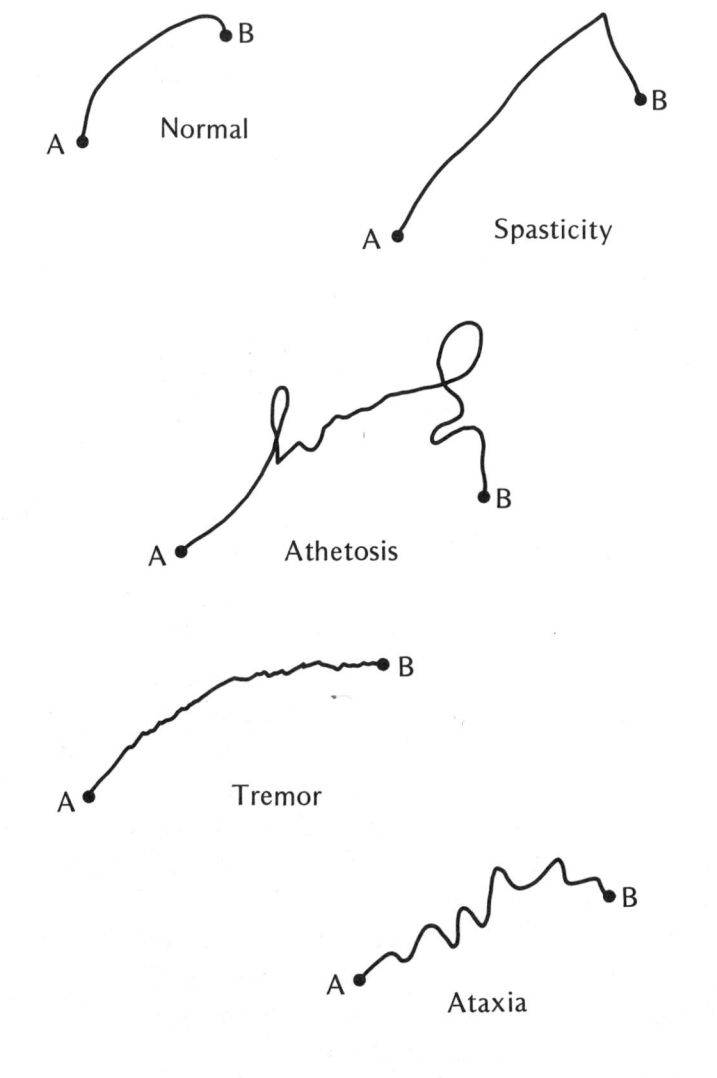

connect two dots, the line wiggles out of control. Children with cerebral palsy due to blood incompatibility usually have the athetoid type of the disorder.

Rigidity usually affects all four limbs. It appears to be a severe form of spasticity. In this form of the disease, the limbs are mostly stiff and unbending.

Persons who walk with a swagger, that is, with feet apart, with twisting of the trunk, and with arms outstretched for balance, may be suffering from ataxia.

Ataxia is the third most common type of cerebral palsy. It is characterized by a lack of balance and a lack of coordination. Children with ataxia fall frequently. Their muscles are flabby and lack good tone. When they try to connect two dots, they usually draw a wavy line from one to the other.

Tremor is a shaking of a limb. In its more usual form, the limb only shakes when the person tries to use it. In cases of tremor, the less common form of the disease, the line connecting two dots is shaky. Stephen Hopkins had the tremor form of cerebral palsy. When he fixed his signature to the Declaration of Independence, it is reported that he said: "Although my hand trembles, my heart does not."

Some children have what doctors call mixed cerebral palsy. Usually these youngsters have both spasticity and athetosis, and it generally involves all four limbs.

Besides the motor disorders caused by cerebral palsy, there are often other associated difficulties. Nearly half the children with cerebral palsy have speech problems caused by lack of control of the muscles necessary to produce sounds. Drooling and difficulty in swallowing also occur when the muscles involved do not function well.

Children with cerebral palsy have more hearing

and sight impairments than those without the disease. Poor hearing is common in athetosis, as is the inability to move the eyes upward. Convulsions or seizures occur most among children with spastic cerebral palsy and among some with athetosis. Mental retardation occurs with more frequency among children with cerebral palsy than in the general population.

Cerebral palsy does not get worse with time, and except in the most severe cases does not lead to reduced life expectancy. But there is no cure for the disease.

The chief treatment is physical therapy. The therapist sets up patterns to train the youngster to move in a controlled, natural way, with good posture and balance. The goal is to eliminate as much of the poor muscle movement as possible. In some few cases, surgery is used to relieve contracted muscles and to correct deformities in the bones caused by the tightened muscles. No drugs have yet been found to relieve the symptoms.

Experiments are now going on to implant brain pacemakers in victims of the disease. With these instruments, doctors hope to control involuntary muscle activity. The super-cold method of cryosurgery is being explored too. Deadening areas of the brain might help to eliminate some of the symptoms of the disease. Researchers are learning more about cerebral palsy as they seek cures, but they have not yet made any really major advances.

Studies show that most people with mild cases of cerebral palsy can lead completely normal lives, no different from the rest of the population. Those with more serious conditions need a somewhat sheltered environment; a job that takes into account their disability and a home where they can be helped. Victims of the very severe forms of the disease may have to live in custodial situations.

EPILEPSY

Sharon is a third grader. She is a happy child, popular with the other children, and a good student. Sharon and the people around her are hardly ever aware that she has epilepsy. Epilepsy is a disorder of the brain and nervous system that results in occasional, sudden, temporary losses of consciousness, called seizures.

Sharon knows that a seizure is coming on when she gets a certain "funny" feeling in her stomach. A few minutes later, she loses consciousness. Her body becomes stiff, as do her arms and legs. Unless she is supported, she falls to the ground. Sometimes she utters a strange-sounding cry as air is forced out of her lungs past the tightened vocal cords.

At first her arms and legs thrash violently. Gradually, though, they become still. Because she is not able to swallow and her lips are moving, she seems to be frothing at the mouth. And for a short time she stops breathing, so her complexion takes on a bluish tint.

Sharon's teacher and the other children in the class know all about the disorder. Every child knows what to do if Sharon gets an attack in school. At the first sign, someone goes for the padded mat in the closet. The two children nearest to Sharon help the teacher lay her down on the mat. They place her on her side, so she will not choke. At the same time, the one nearest the door goes for the nurse.

Within a few minutes the attack is over. Sometimes Sharon comes out of it with nothing more than a headache. Sometimes she sleeps for a while, right on the mat.

Sharon takes medicine that controls the frequency of the attacks. She seldom has these seizures more than once or twice a year. But since Sharon, the other children, and her family know all about epilepsy, it is treated as a matter-of-fact occurrence, without fear or embarrassment.

In primitive times, sudden attacks of epilepsy, called fits or seizures, were thought to be signs of the supernatural. Hippocrates, the ancient Greek who established the first principles of medical science nearly 2500 years ago, called epilepsy "the sacred disease." Others referred to it as "the falling sickness." The word itself comes from the Greek, meaning "seizures."

Today doctors know that about 8 out of every 1,000 children have epilepsy. It is often described as a childhood disease, but it can strike at any age. About 75 percent of the cases start before age eighteen. Approximately half of the children with seizures outgrow them, usually when they reach puberty. Some get other types of seizures after they reach sixteen years or so.

Epilepsy is not believed to be inherited. Only 2 to 5 percent of children with epilepsy are believed to have inherited the disease. But children do seem to inherit the tendency to develop seizures. Most often, however, the disorder can be traced to brain injuries or infection, or other damage to the brain.

There is evidence that one-fourth to half of all cases of epilepsy could be prevented. Checking pregnancy among teenagers would be one way, since teenagers are more likely than others to bear children with epilepsy. Immunization against measles, mumps, and diphtheria can prevent brain damage and seizures that may result from severe cases of these diseases. Using seat belts in cars, wearing helmets while riding motorcycles, or mopeds, and driving at a safe speed can prevent head injuries that might cause epilepsy.

Doctors usually diagnose children with epileptic seizures on the basis of reports given them by parents, teachers, or the youngsters themselves. More is learned about the disorder by means of an EEG (electroencephalogram). In this test the doctors attach electrodes to a number of spots around the skull. The instrument locates and measures the electrical signals that are given off by the cells in the tissues of the brain.

A seizure occurs when some electrical instability triggers an "electrical storm" that spreads over all or part of the brain. By studying the pattern of brain waves that shows up on the EEG, the doctor can sometimes determine the exact site of damage or infection of the brain.

Sharon has the most common and also the most severe type of epilepsy. It is called grand mal, which means "grand sickness." The victim of a grand mal seizure loses consciousness and usually falls. The muscles contract in spasms or convulsions. The person stops breathing regularly, often turning blue in the face. The attack is usually over within two to five minutes. There is no pain, though there is always the danger of being hurt by the fall. Usually, there is no memory of the attack.

A less severe type of epilepsy is called petit mal, or "little sickness." While the grand mal type is called the falling sickness, the petit mal is called the staring sickness. The attack usually lasts five to ten seconds.

During the brief loss of consciousness the person freezes in place, staring fixedly at some point. At the same time, there is usually some fluttering of the eyelids and occasionally the eyes roll up. There are no convulsive movements of the muscles during the attack. In fact, more often than not, observers think the child is just daydreaming. Sometimes a petit mal seizure may be brought on by an exciting event, such as a party or the loss of a loved object.

The psychomotor form of epilepsy is hardest to diagnose. Abnormal electrical signals from just one part of the brain are the cause. They lead to a stiffening or jerking about of one arm or leg, or the arm and leg on the same side. Sometimes it just affects one side of the face or a corner of the mouth, along with the fingers on that side. The attack lasts between two and five minutes.

On occasion, it starts in one place and moves to the other side of the body. That is why it is sometimes called "march" epilepsy. The person does not lose consciousness, but is unable to speak or respond. Restraint during the fit may cause the person to struggle and thrash about. A short period of amnesia often follows.

Doctors can now prescribe from a whole range of anticonvulsive medicines that control epileptic seizures. About 50 percent of the people can eliminate seizures through medication. Another 30 percent can reduce the frequency of the seizures. The remaining 20 percent are hardly helped by any of the present drugs.

Persons subject to epileptic seizures can lead normal lives. Children can attend regular classes and take part in all activities. Adults can work at almost any but a few jobs where there is danger from a momentary lack of consciousness. In most cases, keeping busy and active is most helpful in reducing the frequency of seizures.

Except for the brief duration of a seizure, those with epilepsy need no special help or consideration. One child summed it up very well: "Epilepsy means small periods of time of losing touch. Why should this affect the way a person feels about me, or the way I feel about myself?"

The greatest handicaps to people with epilepsy are still ignorance, fear, and superstition. Until very recently, some states prohibited the marriage of someone with epilepsy, and others allowed those subject to epileptic seizures to be sterilized without consent. Even now, people with epilepsy suffer job discrimination, rejection, and needless embarrassment and guilt.

Actually, most individuals marry and have children who are free of the disorder. About 80 percent are employed at jobs which they handle very well. Their accomplishments are no less significant than the achievements of the famous rulers Alexander the Great and Julius Caesar, the composers Handel and Tchaikowsky, the artist Van Gogh, and the writer Dostoyevsky — all subject to epileptic seizures during their lifetimes.

6 OTHER NERVE AND MUSCLE DISORDERS:

**Multiple Sclerosis
Muscular Dystrophy
Spina Bifida
Polio**

MULTIPLE SCLEROSIS

Multiple sclerosis, or MS, is an incurable, progressive, disabling disease of the central nervous system. It mostly strikes individuals between twenty and forty years of age. Once thought to be rare, it now seems fairly common. There are believed to be about 500,000 victims of multiple sclerosis in America today.

The specific cause of the disorder is not known. But what happens is that the disease attacks small patches of myelin, the insulating substance that makes up the outer covering of many nerve fibers. These small patches of myelin become hard and die. The word sclerosis comes from the Greek word meaning "hard." In the acute phase of the disease, the hard areas are found throughout the central nervous system, hence *multiple* sclerosis.

Nerve impulses to and from the brain have trouble getting past these damaged areas. This interference causes malfunctions in the nervous system.

The symptoms are many and unexpected. They depend on the location of the hardened areas. At first, there may be numbness in parts of the body, double vision, speech difficulties, or prickly sensations ("pins and needles") in the legs. Later, there is often weakness in the knees, loss of balance, and muscle stiffness. Dizziness may follow. Sometimes there is paralysis and loss of bladder or bowel control.

The disease usually progresses slowly. Attack follows attack in an unpredictable way. Symptoms gradually worsen. With each attack there is further disability.

However, many people with MS have periods of remission or "plateauing." That is, long periods of time go by with only an occasional symptom or even general improvement. The entire course of the disease may take twenty-five years or more.

One of the most difficult aspects of the disease is its unpredictability. A person affected with the symptoms does not know if the disease will remain mild, get worse, or get better. No one knows what, if anything, can be done to slow it down or make it go away.

Another distressing symptom of MS is that patients occasionally cry when they do not feel sad, or laugh when they are not particularly happy. The lack of control is due to problems with the complex nervous system. These inappropriate reactions are very hard for some people to handle.

No proven drugs or treatments are yet known that can change the course of MS. Rest and physical therapy help to hold back the damaging effects in the early stages of the disease. The doctors and therapists work on each area of weakness as it shows up. They try to help the patient to walk and remain independent for as long as possible. Prevention of upper respiratory and other infections is very important. Braces are sometimes used to help stabilize limbs.

Many persons with MS continue to work and lead useful lives. They do not permit increasing disability to damage their self-esteem or self-respect. People with MS are able to remain self-sufficient much longer than is generally believed.

MUSCULAR DYSTROPHY

Muscular dystrophy, MD, is a general term for a group of closely related diseases that attack and destroy the muscle fibers of the body. Most types of MD follow a gradual, ever-worsening progression of

This young woman leads a fairly normal life, despite the fact that she has multiple sclerosis.

symptoms. The skeletal muscles of the body, those muscles that move the bones, become weak and waste away.

MD is most common among very young children, mostly boys. At around the age of three, the affected children may begin to show the first symptoms of the most common form of MD. These children find it hard to climb stairs. It is difficult for them to get up from a sitting or lying position. So gradual are these first symptoms that they may not be noticed for months or even years.

As the disease advances, the muscles grow weaker and weaker. The muscles also appear to grow larger. The increase in size is due to the fact that the muscle tissue is being replaced by fat. The enlargement of the muscle is seen mostly in the calves of the legs, and sometimes in the arms.

The muscle weakness leads to inactivity. Inactivity is responsible for even further loss of muscle strength or tone. Frequent overeating compounds the problem. The children often become overweight.

By age ten to twelve, children with MD are sometimes unable to walk. They are confined to a wheelchair, or even to bed. Various deformities of the skeleton are present: The shoulders are thrown back, the spine is curved (scoliosis), and the abdomen protrudes.

A high percentage of these youngsters are mentally retarded. Those afflicted with the disease cannot fight off infections. Death usually follows in the late teens or early twenties from respiratory disease. In some cases, death is caused by failure of the muscles that control the heart and lungs.

Muscular dystrophy is an inherited disease, but the precise cause is unknown. Nor is any cure or treatment for MD yet known. Massive research programs are now under way to learn more.

Some of the symptoms of MD are relieved by physical therapy. The muscles are not exercised or stretched. Rather, they are held in natural, comfortable positions for periods of time. Group games are helpful in keeping up the fullest range of muscle movement. Games that include blowing and shouting aid in maintaining lung capacity. Braces and surgery are used in some cases to give strength to weak muscles and to correct deformities.

Approximately 1 out of every 1,000 children between the ages of three and thirteen suffers from MD. The largest number have the Duchenne form of the disease, which is the most serious.

This type of MD is inherited from the mother, who carries the defective gene. About half the number of sons born to mothers who carry this gene are affected; about half the daughters born to these women also carry the gene. Scientists have a blood test for the Duchenne type of MD. The test tells the mother-to-be whether or not she is carrying the disease. Many cases of MD can be prevented if women with the MD gene decide to adopt rather than have children of their own.

The outlook for a patient with Duchenne-type MD is very dim. Once the diagnosis is made, the child must face the prospect of a steadily worsening condition, increasing dependency, and an early death. Coping with death may produce fear about sleeping in the dark or being alone. These children may express anger toward their mothers, and become resentful about their dependency, especially as adolescents. Often, they are depressed and brood about the future.

Duchenne-type MD has some of the same psychological effects on parents, teachers, doctors, and friends of the victim as all permanent disabling diseases. There is fear and guilt in the early stages of the disease, and anxiety as the disability becomes worse. For brothers and sisters of these children, there may be the fear that they caused the disease by wishful thinking or as punishment for their bad behavior. They may be fearful of getting the same disease. In the late phases of the disease, there is never-ending work — dressing, feeding, bathing, toileting — caring for the victim of this severe form of MD. There is the struggle of helping the adolescent come to terms with the disease and, finally, the strain of dealing with imminent death.

The facio-scapulo-humeral type of MD is a milder, less common form of the disease. It is inherited from either parent and affects both girls and boys. The symptoms first appear around the adolescent years or the early twenties. This form of MD usually strikes the muscles of the face, shoulder, and upper arms in the beginning stages. There may be some difficulty in whistling or drinking through a straw, at first, or difficulty in raising the arms over the head. This form of MD progresses very slowly. Even though its results are disabling, it seldom shortens the person's life.

The limb-girdle form of MD is also inherited, but only when both parents carry the defective gene. It occurs between the ages of ten and fifty. Most cases, though, start between thirty and fifty years of age. Males and females are affected equally.

The muscle weakness usually appears in the shoulders or around the pelvis. The progress of the disease varies, from quite slow to fairly rapid. Sometimes there is little muscle destruction, and the person is able to reach an advanced age without serious impairment. Other times, the damage is quickly done, making it extremely difficult for the patient to carry on his or her regular routine.

Professionals who deal with victims of MD act as though a cure will be found tomorrow. They do not give way to despair. They try to make the person's life as full and satisfying as the physical condition will allow. As much education and physical education therapy as possible is provided. A rich mixture of experiences in growing, learning, and enjoying is most important.

SPINA BIFIDA

Spina bifida literally means "open spine." It is a condition that starts to develop in the fetus before birth. In this disease, the back parts of the backbones (vertebrae) fail to close properly. This deformity is the most serious and most handicapping condition in children. It is the most common birth defect after cerebral palsy.

There are three main conditions that can develop from an opening in the spine. The mildest condition is spina bifida occulta. One or more of the vertebrae which make up the spinal column are not completely formed. The condition is usually not detected at birth or during childhood. There is no deformity or misplacement of the spinal cord. The danger is that the spinal cord, inside the spinal column, will become infected. Serious infection is usually controlled by antibiotics.

Meningocele is a more serious condition. Here part of the covering of the spinal cord, though not the cord itself, comes out of the spinal column. It forms a small, skin-covered bump, or sac, on the child's spine, about the size of a walnut. The spinal cord is in its normal place and is usually not affected. There is no paralysis with meningocele. The only danger, as with spina bifida occulta, is of infection.

The most common and most damaging of the spina bifida conditions is myelomeningocele (*myelo* is cord, *meningo* is covering of the cord, and *cele* is sac). With this deformity, the spinal cord and the covering both come out through the opening in the spine. The sac that forms may be as large as a grapefruit. It may only be partly covered with skin, and spinal fluid may leak out through the thin membrane which covers it. With this condition, many disabilities usually result.

Permanent paralysis of all or part of the leg muscles is part of myelomeningocele. The amount and extent of paralysis depends on the level of the opening in the spine. The higher the opening, the greater the paralysis.

Because of the full or partial paralysis in the lower limbs, these bones are deformed. Common deformities are dislocated hip, club foot (the foot is bent downward and inward, so the person only walks on tiptoe or on the outside of the feet), rocker-bottom foot (opposite of club foot, the foot is turned up and out creating extremely flat feet), and various defects of the trunk such as a curved spine (scoliosis), humpback (kyphosis), or swayback (lordosis).

Children with myelomeningocele lose all feeling in the lower part of the body. Since they do not feel pain, burns, freezing, or pressure, youngsters with spina bifida are taught to check frequently for skin irritations. The damage to the spinal cord also affects the child's ability to control muscles of the bladder and bowel.

About 90 percent of children with myelomeningocele have water on the brain (hydrocephalus). The spinal fluid cannot circulate properly, and collects in cavities around the brain. This forces the skull to enlarge, which gives this condition its name. It also squeezes the brain cells, which leads to mental retardation.

These various forms of spina bifida occur when the spinal column does not develop completely and close during the first thirty days of pregnancy, as is normal. Perhaps it is due to a virus infection. The cause is not known.

Spina bifida is an inherited disease. It is caused by the interaction of genes from both parents and certain conditions in the environment of the developing fetus. All in all, about 2 out of every 1,000 children born have spina bifida, with slightly more girls affected than boys.

Up until about thirty years ago, all spina bifida children died soon after birth. The usual causes of death were hydrocephalus, an infection at the spinal gap, or an infection of the kidney caused by a backup of urine.

New medical treatments now offer much more hope to the spina bifida infant. Very soon after birth, sometimes within twenty-four hours, surgeons operate to close up the opening in the spine. Although this does not necessarily prevent the paralysis or other disabling conditions, it protects against infection, which could be fatal. In another operation, a plastic tube is inserted into the skull to drain the fluid into either the heart or abdomen. This shunt relieves the pressure on the brain cells and on the bones of the skull.

Later operations are used to correct deformities of the skeletal system. They make it possible for the youngster with this disease to lead a more normal life. They also prevent further damage to the bone structure. Doctors fit the patient with special shoes and with full-body braces to support weak or paralyzed muscles. The youngsters can walk, either unaided or with crutches.

Children with spina bifida are always in and out of hospitals. It is not surprising that they are often lonely and depressed. Family life is difficult. The parents' first reactions are usually shock and rejection, followed by strong feelings of guilt. The great demands on the family's resources of time, attention, and money create further stress and anxiety.

Youngsters who have loving, supportive families and good school programs can develop to their fullest potential. Good progress depends on how well the school recognizes the special needs of such children. Are typewriters available? Spina bifida youngsters have trouble controlling their hands. Are thick pencils handy for their use? Are times and places set apart for them to rest? These children tire easily. And, most important, do the teachers understand the problems of the child with spina bifida and also realize that they are dealing with a feeling, thinking person?

One teacher put it this way: "A spina bifida child with a urine bag, a shunt, and crutches, is still, remarkably, a child with the same needs and sensitivities of any child and capable of responding to an environment that is rich with people and things."

POLIO

Polio (poliomyelitis) is a virus infection of the central nervous system. The disease strikes at the motor cells of the spinal cord that control movement. It is contagious, and is spread when viruses from the infected person enter the victim's body through the mouth.

Until the 1960s, polio was widespread and the most dreaded of all childhood diseases. Since then, two types of polio vaccine have been introduced. They have almost completely eliminated the disease. Still, some children do not receive the vaccine, and cases are beginning to re-occur. For this reason, researchers continue to study the disease. Therapists and teachers are trying to find better ways to help the victims of polio.

The disease occurs most often in children between four and fifteen years of age. People of all ages, however, are susceptible. It often begins with symptoms similar to those of a common cold — fever, sore throat, stiff neck, headache, upset stomach, and sore muscles. In mild forms of the disease, the symptoms disappear in about twenty-four hours before it is even recognized as polio.

In more severe attacks, the symptoms do not go away. Instead, they grow worse. The neck and back become stiff. The muscles are tender. The infected parts of the spinal cord cut off impulses to muscles that move the arms and legs and other parts of the body. Paralysis sets in. If breathing muscles are affected, a respirator is needed to replace the body's breathing mechanism.

The amount of paralysis depends on the amount of damage to the motor cells by the polio virus. The result may range from weakened muscles in an arm or leg to complete paralysis. During the early, acute phase of the disease, treatment includes bed rest, exercises to improve the tone of affected muscles, and hot packs to relax the tightened muscles. Later, physical therapy helps to build up strength in the muscles. Where they can help, braces are fitted and patients are taught how to walk with canes or crutches.

Franklin Delano Roosevelt is an inspiring example of one who overcame a severe attack of polio. He went on to become president and to lead our nation through a difficult time in its history.

FDR suffered the first symptoms of polio on August 9, 1921. By August 11th, he could neither stand nor walk. He felt great pain in the muscles of his back and legs. After the acute phase was over, both legs were completely paralyzed, and the muscles in his hands and back were badly weakened.

Many people, including his mother, urged him to give up his political career. But his wife Eleanor urged him to carry on. With her help, FDR decided to fight the disease. His doctors and therapists prescribed a daily routine of exercises. He built up the strength in his hands and his back. He swam to exercise his legs. With leg braces and canes he was able to walk.

In 1932, after a strenuous campaign, FDR was elected President of the United States. An active, busy chief executive, he brought America out of the Depression and guided it to victory through most of World War II. The vast majority of the American people never realized the severity of his disability.

MS, MD, spina bifida, and polio are not the only causes of paralysis. Accidents, especially, that damage the spine or central nervous system, can also lead to permanent paralysis.

Paralysis is often described by the number of limbs that are involved. The most common terms are paraplegia, which refers to paralysis of both legs, and quadriplegia, which refers to paralysis of both arms and legs. In popular usage, though, paraplegia denotes both conditions.

The number of paraplegics is increasing every year. In the past, paraplegics either died in infancy (if they were born paralyzed) or within a year after the onset of paralysis. The usual cause of death was an infection in one of the organs of elimination, such as the kidney or bladder. Advances in medical science have made it possible to prevent or control these infections, and to lengthen the life of the paraplegic.

One of the outstanding pioneers in caring for paraplegics is Dr. Ludwig Guttman. In 1944, he opened a Spinal Injuries Center at the Stoke Mandeville Hospital in England to care for war casualties with spinal damage. The usual way to care for paraplegic patients was to keep them flat on their backs in plaster casts. Bedsores and kidney infections developed, and sometimes caused the patients' deaths.

Dr. Guttman devised treatments that required the patient to exercise the healthy parts of the body. Patients were made to care for their own needs, became mobile with wheelchairs or crutches, and built up strength by standing with parallel bars. Vocational training continued even while patients were in bed. And a whole range of sports and other activities was introduced for their mental and physical well-being.

Out of Dr. Guttman's work have come many exciting advances in this field. Paraplegics now actively pursue archery, table tennis, and weight lifting. They take part in basketball, polo, and even football. With just slight modifications of the rules, paraplegics speed their wheelchairs up and down the courts, passing and shooting the ball, proving that sports belong to them just as they do to the non-disabled. Bowling is particularly popular with paraplegics. There are many leagues. Players especially like the fact that bowling does not require any modifications of the rules.

Wheelchair sports are very widespread. The "Paralympics" is an annual international sports event that started in England. It draws contenders from all over the world. On the schedule at the National Wheelchair Games, held in cities throughout the United States, are relays, dashes, javelin throwing, shot putting, and ping pong.

Increasing numbers of paraplegics now go to school and work, get married, and have families. They seek out the best medical and psychological help. They follow the instructions of professionals who are highly trained and skilled.

Often successful adjustment means repeating over and over again movements and exercises that will return strength to their weak muscles and prevent their unused muscles from wasting away. It means a willingness to venture into new areas — to get a car with hand controls, to travel near and far, to work at jobs that have long been denied to paraplegics.

There are no paraplegics who have not had to work hard to live a better life. But most feel it is worth the struggle for a chance to fulfill one's goals.

7

BONE AND JOINT DISORDERS:

Amputations
Scoliosis
Arthritis

Bones support the body. They are moved by muscles and tendons. The way they move determines how the body moves.

Bones also protect the vital organs of the body. They store essential minerals. They produce red blood cells and certain kinds of white blood cells which cleanse the blood of harmful substances.

Strong, flexible ligaments tie the bones together to form joints. The joints permit the body framework to move. The amount of motion and the kind of motion in a joint depends on the structure of the bone ends, the space between these ends, and the way the bones are tied together by the ligaments.

Bones form long before birth. They are living organs that need certain chemical substances in order to grow and develop. Permanent impairments of the bones and joints may be present from birth or may occur as a result of accidents or disease after birth.

AMPUTATIONS

Henry ("Hank") Viscardi was born without legs or feet. The stumps extended only to where the knees should have been. The doctors call it a congenital amputation. For some unknown reason, his legs had failed to develop before birth.

For the first six years of his life, Hank was in and out of hospitals. A number of operations made it possible for him to move about on the stumps of his legs. He was also fitted with padded boots that he said looked like boxing gloves.

Since his legs were so short, Hank's arms reached almost to the ground. Viscardi recalls in his autobiography how some children in the neighborhood used to call him "ape man."

Hank was always interested in sports. He was always a good swimmer. In high school, he became manager of the basketball team. He helped support his family by refereeing high school basketball games, and reporting on school athletics for *The New York Times*.

After graduating from high school, Viscardi entered Fordham University to study science. He struggled to pay his tuition and other expenses by working as a busboy, library assistant, and switchboard operator. Earnings from these various jobs, however, were not enough to keep up with his college costs, so he had to drop out.

When he was twenty-six years old, Hank Viscardi met Dr. Robert Yanover, an orthopedic surgeon. (Orthopedic surgeons operate to restore or preserve the bones of the body.) Dr. Yanover put the young man in touch with George Dorsch, a maker of artificial limbs. Not only did Dorsch fit Hank with artificial legs, but he trained him to walk on them. It took a long time before Viscardi mastered the art of walking with his new legs. But then he did not stop there. He learned how to run, and even how to dance.

Not long after, Viscardi opened a small workshop that only employed workers with severe disabilities. The enterprise grew into a large factory, now called Abilities, Inc. The firm employs and trains hundreds of people for industry. They produce and sell products worth millions of dollars every year.

Viscardi later founded a school which serves as a model for educating children with serious physical disabilities. It is called the Human Resources School. Children with a host of disabling conditions learn all the usual subjects, along with music, art, and sports such as swimming, bowling, and wheelchair basketball. The aim of this outstanding facility is to help all the children to develop to the limits of their potential.

About 25,000 children and 175,000 adults are missing all or part of one or more limbs. While some are congenital amputees, many lost a limb because of disease or accident. They are said to be acquired amputees. Amputation, congenital or acquired, is a limited disability. It does not affect one's intelligence.

Teddy Kennedy Jr., nephew of the late President John F. Kennedy, had a rare form of cancer in the bones of his right leg. The disease was discovered when he was twelve years old. To prevent the spread of the cancer, surgeons had to amputate his right leg four inches above the knee.

Teddy was fitted with an artificial leg. Not only can he now walk on the leg, but he can play football, baseball, sail, ride his bicycle, and participate in all the sports he always enjoyed. He leads a normal, active life.

Artificial legs and arms are called prostheses. They are now built of light, strong materials. Many are operated by muscular or electrical signals from within the user's body. They are built to resemble natural limbs in size, shape, color, and feel. Physical therapists train those who have lost limbs to use prostheses.

Children can be especially skillful in quickly learning to use artificial limbs. It is sometimes impossible to tell that someone is using a prosthetic device. And artificial arms and hands are usually stronger than natural ones, sometimes capable of doing even more than natural limbs can do.

The most serious problem of amputation can be one of psychological adjustment. Our society places a great premium on the body, whole and beautiful. The loss of a limb is sometimes a most difficult disability for people to accept. But once the disability is accepted, there is no reason for not living a full, rich, and satisfying life.

SCOLIOSIS

Not long ago, the mother of a twelve-year-old girl named Jenny became concerned about her daughter's appearance. She noticed that the girl's right and left hips and her shoulders were not equal in height. From the back, her spine seemed to be curved to the left.

A doctor examined and X-rayed the youngster. The condition was diagnosed as scoliosis, or curvature of the spine.

Scoliosis can affect any part of the spine. In early cases, there is a single curve, like the letter C. In advanced cases, there is often a double curve, more like the letter S.

Scoliosis occurs eight times as frequently in girls around puberty as in boys. In its mild form, it may be caused by one leg being shorter than the other or by faulty posture. The doctor or physical therapist treats these milder forms with special exercises to correct the condition.

Jenny's form was more severe: She had idiopathic scoliosis, or scoliosis of unknown cause. The doctor recommended that Jenny wear a Milwaukee Brace. This metal device reaches from the pelvis to the base of the skull. It applies pressure against the curvature, gradually forcing the spine into good alignment. Jenny needs to wear the brace day and night, with only a short time out each day for bathing and exercise.

At first, Jenny was ashamed to go to school wearing the brace. But her parents bought her some especially nice outfits which concealed the brace better than some of her other clothes. They helped her in other ways to make up for the inconvenience of the brace. With understanding from her teachers and friends, too, she was able to overcome her apprehension. She accepted the fact that she had to wear it.

Before long, she was going to parties and dances, and had resumed all of her previous activities. In fact, she became even more active than before. She began gymnastics and horseback riding. If Jenny wears the brace and continues the exercises for two to three years, the curvature may be corrected. At the very least, it will not worsen.

ARTHRITIS

Rheumatism and arthritis are often thought to be diseases of older people. Yet juvenile rheumatoid arthritis, JRA, strikes children as young as six weeks old.

Rheumatism refers to a whole group of disorders affecting muscles and joints. Arthritis literally means inflammation of the joints. These diseases cause aching, stiffness, and pain, not only in the joints, but in the muscles, ligaments, and tendons as well.

JRA affects about 3 out of every 100,000 children under twelve each year. The most common form of the disease, called polyarticular JRA, presents several symptoms. Usually the joints at the knee, ankles, and wrist are involved. Less often, the neck, fingers, elbows, and shoulders become painful and stiff. The victims also have fever (which reaches 105° or so), a flat pink rash, and blood tests show that they are anemic.

The young victims of JRA feel uncomfortable

most of the time. They move very little and hold their arms and legs bent, since they feel less pain that way. They also hold their necks rigidly for comfort.

Permanent damage sometimes occurs to the joint while the disease is active. The cartilage — the smooth, slippery material at the joints that permits the bones to move freely against each other — may become irritated. The disease hurts because the bones in the joints, stripped of the protective coating of cartilage, grind and scrape against each other. Also, the disease may tighten and scar the muscles and soft tissue around the joint.

Doctors have no way to cure JRA. All they can do is control the inflammation and other effects of the disease. One of the best drugs is aspirin. Many find it hard to believe that such a common non-prescription drug could be so effective. But in some cases, as many as ten tablets or more are taken each day to control the pain.

Another part of the treatment is rest. Weight or pressure on the diseased joints causes more damage. Some physicians insist the child have complete bed rest. Other youngsters are told to use crutches or wheelchairs to avoid straining the joints. In general, going to sleep early and napping or lying down during the day may also help.

Exercise for the stricken joints is very important. Usually physical therapists work with the child to move the inflamed joints once or twice a day. They stretch the muscles and joints to the fullest extent possible, but not so far as to cause further inflammation. Swimming in warm water is soothing. The buoyancy of the water protects the joints from bearing too much weight. Moving through water also increases the strength of the joint.

JRA often affects the personalities of children with the disease. They may become very depressed. For long periods they may seem shy and introverted. Then suddenly, they may act out, and become very angry. This variability of behavior is just as much a part of JRA as the pain in the joints.

In part the personality difficulties are caused by the unpredictable nature of the disease. JRA can come, and then go and never return. Or it can disappear completely, and then return worse than ever. It can last a lifetime, or the child may outgrow it. It may cause little crippling, or it may be severely crippling within a few months.

But its unpredictability also gives reason for hope: The disease is seldom fatal. Further research into the cause and treatment may yet unlock the mysteries of this physically and psychologically damaging disease.

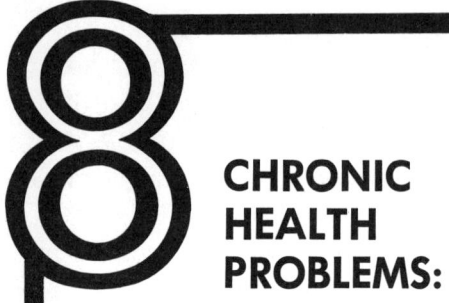
8
CHRONIC HEALTH PROBLEMS:

Hemophilia
Heart Disease
Diabetes
Cystic Fibrosis
Asthma
Anemia

Chronic health problems are those that affect one or more organs of the body and last for a long time; they may even last a lifetime. Among the more widespread chronic conditions of children are hemophilia, heart disease, diabetes, cystic fibrosis, asthma, and anemia. It is estimated that 20 percent of children in the U.S. have some form of chronic illness or handicap.

The chronic diseases pose special problems because they are mostly invisible. You cannot tell that someone has a chronic disease as easily as you can see that someone is paralyzed or missing a limb. Obvious disabilities are often easier to accept than hidden ones.

Chronic diseases may be more difficult to manage than other disabilities. They frequently involve lengthy hospital stays. This causes anxiety and stress for the children, for their parents, and for their siblings. The expenses can be a hardship on the entire family.

Some chronic diseases cause constant and severe pain. Sometimes the pain cannot be controlled by drugs. A number of diseases grow progressively worse with time. Added to these special problems are the psychological, emotional, social, and educational difficulties that accompany every disability.

HEMOPHILIA

Bobby was a cute baby, with blond hair, round rosy cheeks, and bright blue eyes. For the first few months of his life, his parents, Suzanne and Robert Massie, could only think how lucky they were to have such an attractive, happy, healthy baby.

The first hint that something might be wrong came when Bobby was five months old. His uncle had played with him — tossing him up in the air and catching him. All the while Bobby had laughed and had a wonderful time.

Later, Mrs. Massie noticed a dark-colored bruise on Bobby's side, about the size of a marble. She mentioned it to the doctor at Bobby's next check-up. The doctor seemed a bit concerned, and suggested that they take a blood count.

Bobby's mother took him to a lab, where a nurse took a sample of blood by sticking a needle into one of his toes. When they got home, Mrs. Massie found that the child's sock was soaked with blood. The tiny pin prick was still oozing blood. She bandaged it, but the bleeding did not stop. When Mrs. Massie called the doctor, he told her to get Bobby to the hospital for further tests.

In two days, the tests were completed. The diagnosis was in. Bobby had hemophilia, the bleeding disease. His blood lacked certain factors that caused blood to clot. It took a long time, and sometimes a transfusion of blood containing the missing factor, for Bobby's blood to clot after even the smallest cut or scrape.

Bobby's growing-up years were very difficult. As he started to crawl, stand, and walk, there were inevitable falls and bumps. Each day new dark blue, painful bruises appeared on his body, showing that there was bleeding under the skin. There were frequent treatments and blood transfusions.

As Bobby got older and more active, the number of emergencies increased. Soon he was receiving over one hundred transfusions of blood a year.

One of the most serious crises occurred when Bobby was dancing at home, with his mother. His left knee began to bother him. It swelled and became very painful.

Mrs. Massie quickly called the doctor. He suggested that she wait an hour, and see if the swelling and pain would go down. But the knee grew worse. By the time they got to the doctor's office, Bobby's knee joint was the size of a small melon.

Worse than the swelling was the fact that the knee had become locked into place. Bobby could not move it from its bent position. It took three months and thirty transfusions of blood to stop the bleeding entirely. And it took seven years in casts and braces before Bobby could move his left leg again.

Now Bobby Massie is a young man. At eighteen years of age he entered Princeton University. Photography, music, sports, and science are among his chief interests. There are still times when the bleeding starts in one of his joints or somewhere else in his body. Sometimes he needs immediate medical care, bed rest, time in a wheelchair, cast or braces, or a transfusion.

But Bobby accepts his disability. "I am pleased with the way I am," he says, "for I feel that I have the potential within me to lead an even more beautiful life than I have up to now."

Hemophilia has been called "the disease of royalty." The disease appears in the history of the ruling families of England, Germany, Spain, and Russia, as well as in the ancient lands of Egypt and Babylon. It is a lifelong bleeding condition caused by an abnormality in blood clotting. The big danger is not that the patient will bleed to death from a cut. Rather it is that internal bleeding will badly damage the joints or some vital organs.

Hemophilia is an inherited disease transmitted by the mother. It mostly affects boys. About 11 out of every 100,000 children have the disease.

Ordinary activities put heavy pressure on the joints in the knees, hips, shoulders, and elbows. This causes small bleeding points. In most children, the bleeding stops by itself. But the child with hemophilia continues to bleed, sometimes for hours. The joints swell and hurt. Repeated bleeding results in thickening of the joint lining, leading to inflammation and arthritis. A blow to the head or neck can cause bleeding in the brain or other vital areas.

Care of the child with hemophilia involves setting some limits in activity. In general, children with the disease should not be involved in contact sports such as football or basketball. They should not play baseball or similar sports in which they may be injured by the ball.

Exercise, however, is important for maintaining strong muscles and good joints. Normal physical and social activities are helpful, so far as the illness will allow. Using weights and pulleys and swimming are good physical activities.

To some extent, taking risks is better than being overly cautious. As one child said, "I found the more careful I was, the more I got hurt." Another added, "It's hard to always hear 'no' to everything you would like to do. Sometimes I've landed in the hospital for something I've done — but it was worth it."

In a questionnaire of 1,055 adults with hemophilia, most agreed that the emotional stress in childhood was the worst part of the disease. Children who are overprotected tend to withdraw. Overly cautious children have greater possibilities of bleeding. Children who view themselves as different may hesitate to risk relationships with others.

Hemophilia does not affect intelligence. When children with the disease perform below level in school, it may be because of prolonged absences.

The treatment of children with hemophilia has improved greatly. In the past, bleeding internally or from a cut in the skin had to be treated in the hospital by a blood transfusion. Now, at home, patients are able to administer an injection of precisely the blood factors that are responsible for clotting, the moment that bleeding starts. This avoids complications from uncontrolled bleeding, long hospital stays, and frequent absences from school. It is quite expensive, though, and often imposes a financial burden on the family.

There are no schools for children with hemophilia in the United States or Canada, but some do exist in England and France. Most of those adults with hemophilia who were interviewed hold the opinion that regular schools are best for children with the disease.

Hemophilia is a crippling and life-threatening disorder. It can be controlled with proper medical and social management, however. With a positive outlook, like that of Bobby Massie and his parents, it can even strengthen determination and build character.

HEART DISEASE

Heart disease is the major killer of adults. But do you know that it is also a very dangerous disease among children? Youngsters with the disease are almost

Young hemophiliacs can learn to give themselves the clotting factor, thus allowing them to enjoy many activities once denied them.

always born with a damaged heart. Childhood heart disease, in other words, is nearly always congenital.

The heart of the fetus is formed very early in pregnancy, usually between the third and seventh weeks. What starts out as a straight tube bends, folds, and twists until it becomes the complex structure that we call the heart. In about 600 out of every 100,000 infants, though, something goes wrong in this development. An opening may be left between two parts of the heart that should be closed. Or what should be a wide passageway is either too narrow or is blocked.

Some cases of congenital heart disease are noticed very soon after birth. "Blue babies," so called because of the pale blue tint of their lips and fingernails, suffer from cyanosis, a lack of oxygen in their blood. This condition can appear at any time. It is one of the symptoms of heart disease.

Other symptoms that appear after birth are shortness of breath, excessive tiredness, slow growth and development, occasional fainting, and a deformed chest shape. In some youngsters the disease is not noticed until a doctor listens to the heart through a stethoscope. Sounds, such as a murmur, indicate that that the heart is not working properly.

The treatment depends on the deformity and its seriousness. When the situation is very dangerous, a surgeon may operate at once. The usual procedure is open-heart surgery. Doctors use heart-lung machines to sustain the infant's life while they work directly on the heart to mechanically correct the defect.

In less serious cases, doctors may wait a few years before proceeding with surgery. Many times surgery is not necessary at all, and the condition may be controlled by drugs.

Rheumatic fever is a disease of childhood that sometimes damages the heart. It usually follows an infection somewhere in the body caused by streptococcus bacteria. Rheumatic fever may permanently damage the valves or the lining of the heart.

More deaths are caused by rheumatic fever than by any other disease that affects children of school age. The first attack usually occurs when a child is in the first or second grade. It may then recur any number of times throughout the high school years. Children with rheumatic heart disease must usually limit their physical activity and be under constant medical supervision. Frequently they have a lowered resistance to infection and must take medication, usually penicillin, for many years. Many become easily upset under emotional strain.

Research shows that there is little or no difference in intelligence between children with chronic heart disease and other children. Most of them do best in regular school classes.

Since heart disease is one of the "invisible" disabilities, children with these conditions must make their own adjustments. Pressures from their friends to conform are sometimes hard to resist. One second grader put it very well when he said: "I wish I didn't have any legs, so the other kids could see that I just can't play hard. I'm no sissy!"

The frustrations of chronic heart disease can be even worse for high school students. They are even more concerned with their friends' opinions of them, and want to achieve and maintain status in the group. But the chronically ill have to live within their limitations. By avoiding sustained, vigorous activity, they can live fully and well.

DIABETES

Diabetes is called juvenile diabetes mellitus when it affects children. It is an inherited disease, neither contagious nor infectious. It is not brought on by eating too many sweets, or any other factor in the diet. Diabetes mellitus may appear anytime between early infancy and old age.

With diabetes, the body is unable to digest food properly. This leads to excessive amounts of sugar in the blood and urine. The problem is that the pancreas, one of the organs needed for digestion, does not produce enough insulin, the hormone that lets the cells of the body absorb sugar.

Although diabetes is inherited, it is not present at birth. The first sign of the disease is a rise in the sugar level in the blood and urine. In mild cases, the child at first may have a sore that does not heal, a wound that becomes infected, or a prolonged cold. The symptoms in more severe diabetes are loss of weight, production of large amounts of urine, frequent thirst, and a general feeling of tiredness and weakness.

About 100 out of every 100,000 school children have diabetes. Mostly the onset is sudden and unexpected. There is no cure. Since the cause of the disease is the body's inability to produce insulin, the treatment is to provide the body with that hormone. The insulin is usually extracted from the pancreases of slaughtered cattle.

Insulin taken by mouth would be digested and not effective. Therefore, it is injected into the bloodstream. Most children with diabetes over the age of eight or nine are taught to give themselves daily injections of insulin. They use a special needle with a trigger arrangement that automatically sends the tip of the needle into the skin. Also, they measure the amounts of sugar in their urine daily to be sure that the disease is under control.

Too little insulin can be very dangerous. In such cases, children show the typical symptoms of diabetes. They are tired, weak, thirsty, hungry, urinate often, and show excess sugar in their urine. The treatment is an insulin injection.

Too much insulin on the other hand, can mean that the brain and other organs in the body are not getting enough sugar. The symptoms appear in a matter of minutes. They include headache, nausea, dizziness, blurred vision, a fast heart rate, a cold sweat, and irritability. The treatment here is sweetened fruit juice, soda pop, a hard sucking candy, or any other quick source of sugar.

The amount of insulin to be injected is based on the average diet and the average amount of exercise of the individual. Exercise works like insulin in the body. It burns up excess sugar. Any major change in diet or exercise affects the need for insulin. Illnesses or infections, such as sore throats or bad colds, require slightly more insulin daily.

Some people who develop the disease in adulthood are able to take certain drugs by mouth. If they do not treat the disease correctly, they may suffer attacks of boils and other infections. Diabetes in adults may lead to heart disease and stroke. Also, the person with diabetes is more likely to have eye problems. Diabetes is the third leading cause of blindness in the United States.

Persons who have diabetes should make their own decisions on whether or not to tell others about their condition. In general, it is best not to hide the disability. Do not hesitate to offer someone with diabetes sugar-free drinks and desserts rather than sugary ones. They are accustomed to that. Treat daily insulin injections matter-of-factly. They are as much a part of the routine of persons with diabetes as washing and brushing their teeth. With correct diet, exercise, and insulin people with diabetes can live long and productive lives.

CYSTIC FIBROSIS

Cystic fibrosis (CF) is an inherited disease. About 70 out of every 100,000 infants are born with this disorder. It occurs mostly among the white population, rarely among blacks or Orientals. It is the most common cause of death in children due to an inherited disease.

In CF, various organs of the body, including the lungs, pancreas, stomach, intestines, and liver, secrete an abnormal, thick, sticky mucus. The symptoms vary from case to case. There are frequently colds and coughs that may last for long periods of time. Often these children develop pneumonia and bronchitis. As a result of CF, the pancreas cannot secrete enzymes needed to digest food properly. Consequently, the children have large bulky stools and frequent bowel movements, as well as unusually large appetites.

Doctors usually diagnose CF by measuring the salt level in the patient's sweat, the so-called "sweat test." An especially high level of salt may indicate CF. Children with CF often have big chests because their lungs are blocked with mucus, allowing air into the sacs but not out. They may also have big abdomens because of gas in the stomach and intestines. Thin arms and legs are also common because the disease prevents the digestive system from absorbing the necessary elements in the food.

There is no known cure for CF, but there are several treatment methods that control the disease. For those whose pancreases are blocked by mucus, substitute material from animal pancreases are prescribed. To lighten the burden on the organ, fatty foods — peanut butter, potato chips, creams, and all foods fried in oil — must be avoided. Since the body does not always absorb all the needed vitamins, additional vitamins are often given. To replace the salt lost in their sweat, children with CF take salt tablets in hot weather, especially when they are very active.

The main concern in treating CF is to keep the lungs free of mucus, and hence of infection. Antibiotics are very important.

Sometimes the child is held at various angles, and clapped on the chest to shake loose the mucus. The child may have to breathe in a chemical mist to make the mucus more liquid. Antibiotics may also be taken into the lungs this way. Breathing exercises, posture exercises, and a daily routine of running are also helpful treatments.

CF children often have difficulty breathing and cough a great deal. The disease is not contagious, though. No one can "catch" the cough of a child with CF. In fact, CF children *should* cough, since it helps to clear the lungs.

In general, the less attention paid to the coughing the better. Pill-taking for the digestive problems should also be overlooked. Nor should any mind be paid to the frequent visits to the toilet, or to the need for second and third helpings at mealtimes. These are all part of the disease.

In the past, most CF victims died at an early age, usually of heart and lung complications. As treatment methods have improved, the life span has lengthened to the late teens or early twenties. With care, most persons with CF live close to normal lives and take part in almost all activities.

Children with CF usually do well in school. It is not that they are any smarter than other children. But they often spend more time on school-related work.

As symptoms worsen, however, hospitalization becomes more frequent. There is depression, fear, and all the other effects on the personality of having a fatal disease.

ASTHMA

Asthma is a chronic disease that causes people to breathe with great difficulty, to wheeze when they breathe, to be short of breath, and to cough frequently. The condition results from a narrowing of the bronchial tubes through which air passes to and from the lungs. As the air goes through the narrowed tubes, it produces whistling noises, which are heard as the wheezes of asthma.

Nearly two million youngsters have asthma — about 2½ percent of all children. Of the chronic diseases, it is the one that causes the highest percentage of school absences.

The causes of asthma are not too well understood. In part, it is an allergy. People with asthma have attacks when they are exposed to substances, called allergens, that are harmless to others. The most common allergens, particularly for young children, are milk, eggs, nuts, chocolate, and wheat flour. Some allergens that are inhaled include pollen from plants, house dust, and dust from such things as wool, feathers, and animal fur. Polluted air and extreme cold can also bring on asthma attacks. And people who already have asthma sometimes have attacks brought on by emotional strain.

None of the allergens, though, will lead to asthma without an inherited tendency toward the disease. Almost everyone who has asthma has parents or close relatives who also have allergies.

Asthma can strike at any age. It usually starts as a single, short, mild spell of coughing and wheezing. As time goes on, other attacks follow, more and more frequently, becoming increasingly severe. The attacks usually start with a dry cough. During the attack itself, the person is forced to stop all activities. He or she hunches the shoulders forward to make breathing easier. There is a struggle for every breath. There is also the wheezing sound, and a worried, anxious expression on the face. The attack can come right after exposure to the allergens or emotional upset, or it can come many hours later. It can last for a few minutes, or up to many hours.

The course of the disease, too, varies from person to person. It may disappear in time, it may stay the same, or it may worsen.

Although there is no known cure for asthma, doctors do have several ways of treating the disease. To avoid the allergens in the air that bring on attacks, they suggest staying away from furry pets, woolen blankets, and rugs or drapes, for example.

Once doctors find the specific allergens responsible for an attack, they may inject the asthmatic person with gradually increasing amounts of these substances until the patient builds up a tolerance for them. To prevent or relieve attacks, doctors prescribe medicines that relax the muscles of the lungs and bronchial tubes.

In general, people with asthma lead lives as normal as possible. They avoid the allergens that make them sick. They avoid endurance sports (racing, basketball, soccer), and take part in those sports that require short bursts of energy (baseball, swimming). When an attack comes, they generally sit down, take any medicine that their doctor has prescribed, and rest without any fuss or bother until they are breathing easily again.

ANEMIA

Anemia is a condition in which the red-cell part of the blood is unable to carry sufficient oxygen to the body's tissues. Various factors may be responsible.

One kind of anemia occurs because the child's body does not produce enough blood. Therefore, red blood cells, which normally make up over half the volume of the blood, are in short supply. Too little blood may stem from poor nutrition, or from an imbalance in the body's endocrine system.

Anemia may also be caused by conditions in the body which destroy the red blood cells. Some are inherited conditions; others are acquired later in life. Some are chronic and permanent; others last only short periods of time.

One of the most serious and dangerous forms of the disease is sickle cell anemia. Sickle cell anemia is an inherited form of anemia. It occurs almost entirely among the black population. About 1 in 12 black Americans is carrying the trait for the disease; 1 out of 500 has sickle cell anemia.

The name comes from the shape that the red blood cells take on in the disease. Rather than being round, like normal red blood cells, they are narrow, rather like sickles. Sickle-shaped cells are not able to carry enough oxygen to the tissues of the body. The sickle cells are also very stiff. Occasionally they form a "log jam" in a small blood vessel. This blocks the flow of blood to some part of the body. Pain and swelling often result.

All persons with anemia are generally weak and pale. Often they are dizzy, short of breath, nervous, and lack strength and endurance. Many children who have forms of anemia show little desire to be active or to play with others.

Sickle cell anemia presents some special problems. The "log jams" mostly harm the bones, the intestines, the spleen, the liver, the gall bladder, the brain, and the lungs. Swelling and pain may be present in the hands and feet, in the abdomen, or in the chest. If the brain is affected, there can be paralysis in an arm or leg, and in serious cases the child falls into a coma.

The treatment for anemia depends on the form of the disease. If the cause is a dietary deficiency, extra iron or vitamin supplements can help. For anemia due to basic problems within some system of the body, drugs, blood transfusions, or even surgery may be necessary. Vigorous exercise usually needs to be avoided. Exercise increases the body's need for oxygen, which the cells are not able to supply. Colds and other infections must be treated at once by a doctor.

Children with anemia may lack the stamina for physical activity. They may seem to withdraw from social contacts. Some feel inadequate. Their symptoms isolate and frustrate them. The disabling effects of anemia seem to rise and fall, leaving them helpless and confused at times. Reduced activity may limit the range of their experience, and slow down their progress in school.

It is up to medical science to find the causes, treatments, and cures to these baffling, debilitating chronic diseases. But until then, there is much that can be done by those persons who come in contact with the sufferers.

Each child with a chronic illness must be appreciated for his or her strengths — never to be pitied, never to be felt sorry for. As Bobby Massie said, speaking of his years in bed, on therapy tables, and in hospital emergency rooms: "I knew that I was different. What disturbed me was that somehow to be different was to be wrong, was to be out of place, was to be rejected."

9

SENSORY IMPAIRMENTS:

Blindness
Deafness
Multiple Handicaps

Your sense organs are like receiving stations that pick up messages from outside. Your eyes take in images of things and people, of pictures and written words. Your ears catch noises and the sounds of speech. Your tongue detects tastes. Your nose accepts various smells. Your skin and your muscles receive sensations of touch, of pressure.

Sense organs translate these messages into nerve impulses. The impulses travel along sensory nerves to the brain. Here they are interpreted. Your brain helps you recognize people, understand words, taste salt, smell flowers, and in general be aware of what is going on around you.

Sometimes something goes wrong with the receiving stations, especially with the eyes or the ears. Sometimes something goes wrong along the nerve pathway that carries the signals from the sense organs to the brain so that the signals do not reach the brain accurately. Or, something goes wrong with some part of the brain itself. When something goes wrong with the sensory apparatus you lose some of your awareness of the world around you.

All people learn by taking in information through the senses. When one or another of the senses is not able to receive this information, intellectual, emotional, and personality growth may be hampered.

There is no automatic compensation for lack of vision or hearing. The blind do not hear better or have a better sense of smell because they are blind. The deaf do not see better or have a better sense of touch because they are deaf. Instead, people with the loss of one of the senses usually work very hard to make better use of the remaining senses. Many people manage very well though they lack one or more of the senses. They show that it is not the number of senses that count, but the way in which they are used.

BLINDNESS AND VISUAL IMPAIRMENT

Charlie Boswell was halfback on the top-ranked University of Alabama football team. Sports writers rated him as one of the top college athletes. Right after graduation he was hired to play professional baseball for the Atlanta Crackers.

But Charlie was only able to finish one season with the Atlanta club, when he was drafted into the Army at the beginning of World War II. Charlie entered the Army as a private, and worked himself up to the rank of captain in the tank corps.

On November 30, 1944, Captain Boswell and his tank were advancing slowly in Germany, facing heavy rifle and bazooka fire. A shell hit the tank, starting a fire in the grease and oil of the tread. Boswell was severely wounded with fragments of steel in his face, head, and chest. Although the doctors performed many operations to remove the metal and repair the damage to Boswell's eyes, they were not able to restore his vision. The young captain was told that he would never see again.

Boswell went through a long period of despair and discouragement. Then, with the same determination to win that had made him such an outstanding athlete, he decided to fight his way back.

Boswell learned how to manage his everyday tasks of dressing, washing, and eating. He learned to read braille, and gather other information by touch. He learned to get around without a dog or a cane, neither of which he wanted to use.

Sports, though, remained the biggest thing missing from his life. One day in the hospital, golf pro Kenny Gleason suggested that Boswell play golf. At first, Boswell thought it was a cruel joke. But he went along with Gleason.

Before too long, Boswell was getting off drives of 200 and 250 yards. Gleason helped him improve his stance, his grip, and his rhythm. He guided Boswell by placing the club against the ball. For putting on the green he rattled the pin in the cup. Boswell had the trained athlete's instinct for hitting the ball expertly and accurately.

In a few years, Boswell became a pro golfer on the blind golfers' championship circuit. Six times in eight years he won the American championship. He became the world's first blind golf champion.

Not only did Boswell triumph in sports, but he also succeeded in business. While playing professional golf, he rose from salesman to manager and then owner of his own flourishing business in downtown Birmingham, Alabama. To Boswell, "Blindness isn't a handicap. It's just an inconvenience."

Loss of vision varies from complete loss, as in the case of Charlie Boswell, to partial loss. About 1 child out of every 1,000 is either blind or partially sighted. The blind are not able to read printed words, with or without assistance of special glasses. The partially sighted can read print with glasses or other magnification.

The eye has often been compared to a camera taking pictures. Light enters the eye through the cornea, which is like a lens. It focuses the image on the back of the eye or retina, which is like the film. The optic nerve takes the image from the retina to the brain to be given meaning, just as the film is developed so the picture can be seen.

But the eye is far more complicated and more

delicate than any camera. It is a living organ made up of tissues, vessels, and muscles. There are many conditions, diseases, or accidents that can damage all or part of the eye and cause visual impairments of varying severity. For children between the ages of five and fifteen, accidents are the single greatest cause of blindness.

The most common visual problems are nearsightedness (myopia), farsightedness (hyperopia), and astigmatism. When the eyeball is too long, light comes to a focus in front of the retina; the person is nearsighted. When the eyeball is too short, the light comes to a focus behind the retina; the person is farsighted. When the cornea is not smoothly curved in all directions, some light is focused in front and some behind the retina; the person has astigmatism.

These conditions are usually discovered after a youngster reads a Snellen chart, and has been examined by the eye doctor. In all but the most severe cases, the doctor prescribes either eyeglasses or contact lenses. They help the cornea to focus the light directly onto the retina.

About 1 to 2 percent of all children have eyes that do not face in the same direction or do not move together. This condition, called strabismus or cross-eyes, is often found in children with cerebral palsy. It can lead to double vision or the loss of vision in one eye. If the condition is treated, either by glasses, exercises, or surgery before the child is five or six years of age, it is usually corrected. Later treatment is much more difficult.

Conditions that affect the retina account for more than 25 percent of all blindness in this country. Thousands more suffer disability from these diseases, but are not blind.

Glaucoma is a disease in which there is a build-up of pressure from fluid inside the eye. One form occurs within the first year of life, another between the ages of six and twelve. The most common type, usually inherited, affects people forty years of age or older.

Children show the first symptoms of the disease when they are annoyed by any bright light, their eyes tear a lot, and the usually clear cornea becomes clouded. The danger of glaucoma is that the increased pressure will damage the cornea. This leads to blindness. The treatment, depending on the case, is either medicated drops or surgery to reduce the pressure.

A cataract is a clouding up of the cornea. It can be caused by a blow to the eye. It is also associated with juvenile diabetes mellitus or Down's syndrome (a form of mental retardation). It occurs frequently in infants born to mothers who had German measles during the first three months of pregnancy. Usually the cataract must be removed surgically. Then the child is given eyeglasses or contact lenses to insure good vision.

Visual impairment or blindness may also be caused by serious infections of the eye, disease or damage to the optic nerve or central nervous system, and the growth of tumors in or around the eye.

Children who are born blind do not know, at first, that they are different from most other children. Their parents, though, need to help them get in touch with the outside world. They must teach the infants to listen, to touch, to move about, and to try new experiences. Above all, they must try to help them develop their memory and their other senses.

Since blind youngsters rely heavily on the spoken word for information and for communication, parents and siblings should talk a lot to them. They need to describe the many things in the environment that the youngsters cannot learn about by touching. Helping blind children to develop the ability to express themselves is a necessity. It is particularly important that those who are blind be able to explain their needs to others. By providing a stimulating environment, parents help their blind children avoid such annoying habits as turning the head back and forth quickly, rolling the eyes, and poking and rubbing their eyes.

Some people say that blind people develop a sixth sense, have superior hearing, and can recognize color by touch. All of these are myths. It would be helpful if they were true — but they are not.

What is true is that most blind people use their other senses better than most sighted people. They train themselves to be more attentive to sound. They learn to "see" with their hands or feet. Telling a red blouse from a blue one is a matter of touch, and remembering how each one feels. Getting around the house — from the tile floor in the kitchen to the carpeted hall to the wooden floor in the bedroom — is a matter of listening to and feeling the different surfaces. A man or woman can take the right bill out of a wallet because when they put them in, they fold the one-dollar bills one way, the five-dollar bills another, and so on.

Those who have a partial loss of vision can sometimes read books and papers printed with especially large type. The only way the blind can read is when the material is printed in braille. This method of read-

This braille watch allows the blind to tell time.

ing by touch was invented by Louis Braille, who had been blind since the age of three. It is based on a "cell" of six raised dots on paper, three dots high and two dots across. Each pattern of raised dots represents a letter, number, or punctuation mark.

Once people learn the braille code, they can read anything printed in braille by sliding their fingertips lightly across the cells. Readers average over one hundred words per minute, about half the speed of an average sighted reader.

The braillewriter is a useful six-key machine that looks like a typewriter. It "types" braille. Braille is written by hand using a stylus and metal plate.

New computerized reading machines are now available to help the blind and the partially sighted. Miniature TV cameras automatically show a whole page of a book, magazine, or newspaper on a TV screen, much larger and brighter than the original. Another device "reads" an entire printed page and instantly transcribes it into braille.

The optacon is a small electronic camera held in one hand. When it is focused on printed words, it translates the letters into sharp pulsations on a finger of the other hand. A printing process is being developed that will print words and pictures, too, in relief above the pages, so that it can be read by touch. There are machines that change words into varying sound patterns. And one experimental device reads words and sentences and says them out loud!

Education has long been the key to independence and self-help for the person who is blind. More than half of all blind children now attend regular public school. Under the new laws, many more may soon enter the educational mainstream.

Very often youngsters who are visually impaired and in the regular classroom are given extra help several times a week by a special teacher who instructs them in braille. The same teacher shows them how to use talking records, which are long-playing recordings of entire books, newspapers, and magazines. These talking books, as well as large print books, are available free of charge from the Library of Congress in Washington, D.C. The tape recorder and typewriter are other tools which blind students use in school. With this help, these young people generally do very well throughout their school careers.

Too many visually handicapped people still sit home with nothing to do. Inactivity can result in lack of coordination, poor muscle tone, and a lack of strength and endurance. But more than that, it results in withdrawal. It limits the full development of the individual. Helen Keller once said, "The curse of the blind is not blindness but idleness."

Increasingly, blind persons can enjoy and take part in a wide range of hobbies and recreational activities. Just as Charlie Boswell found satisfaction in the Blind Golfers' tournaments, there are also more than 1,000 persons who belong to the American Blind Bowling Association. Wrestling, tumbling, swimming, racing, and weight lifting are some other favorite sports among those who are blind.

Bowlers are helped by portable rails which guide them in their starting positions. Racers may be assisted by holding onto a leader that slides along a wire strung along the track.

Baseball, basketball, and soccer games are sometimes played with balls and goals that produce sounds. Music, hiking, and dancing are other social activities that many people who are visually limited enjoy for their own sakes, and because they bring them into touch with others.

The hardest burden blind people bear is the attitude seeing people have toward them. Sometimes they are treated as though they are not able to speak or think for themselves. One blind school teacher says, "The thing I hate most is when I go to a restaurant with friends, the waitress asks them 'Does she want anything?' as if I weren't even there."

If you meet a blind person you know, start off by mentioning your name. Shake hands when the other person extends a hand to you. When you enter a room in which a blind person is alone, tell him or her when you enter. Also, say something when you leave.

Remember that blind is not deaf. Don't shout or raise your voice when speaking to a blind person. Also, blind is not dumb. If you have a question for the blind person, ask that person, not his or her companion. Don't avoid using words such as "see" or "blind" if they fit. Feel free to talk about blindness if both of you feel comfortable about it. Let common sense and your own sensitivity guide you.

DEAFNESS AND HEARING LOSS

All sound is vibration. When the ear works as it should, the vibrations are captured by the outer ear, and are directed through the ear canal to the eardrum. As these vibrations bounce against the eardrum, they cause it to vibrate. The eardrum, in turn, sets the three tiny bones of the middle ear into vibration, which causes the oval window leading to the inner ear to vibrate. This starts the fluid inside the inner ear vibrating. Nerve endings lining the inner ear change the vibrations into impulses of electricity, which pass through the auditory nerve to the brain. Here the impulses are translated into sound.

Each part of the ear is subject to damage, either before birth, by disease, or through an accident. Many of these types of damage can weaken, distort, or destroy hearing.

An estimated 20,000,000 Americans, or 1 out of every 10 people, have some degree of hearing loss. According to the National Health Survey, about 11.5 million persons have a serious hearing loss.

There are two basic kinds of hearing loss. In a conductive hearing loss, the loudness or intensity of the sounds reaching the inner ear is too low for the sounds to be heard. People with this type of hearing loss are said to be hard of hearing.

The major cause of conductive hearing loss is a serious infection of the middle ear, the space between the ear canal and the inner ear. Other causes are malformations or diseases that strike some part of the ear. In any case, sound vibrations are blocked before they reach the inner ear. Conductive or middle-ear deafness usually appears at birth or at an early school age. This is when children are particularly susceptible to upper respiratory infections.

Only rarely does medical or surgical treatment cure children who are born hard of hearing. But some structural faults in the middle ear may be correctable. In the past few years, an operation known as stapes mobilization has helped to restore hearing to many people. In this operation, the surgeon lays back the eardrum, and with the aid of a special microscope loosens the stapes bone, one of the three tiny bones of the middle ear, from the oval window. This is minor surgery that usually requires only twenty-four to thirty-six hours in the hospital and has a high rate of success.

Most people with conductive hearing loss get normal or near-normal hearing through the use of a hearing aid. One type of hearing aid is really a miniature public address system. The user wears a small microphone and amplifier behind the ear or hidden in the frames of eyeglasses, with a receiver placed in the ear canal.

The microphone picks up the vibrations, the amplifier makes them louder, and the receiver plays the louder sound back for the users to hear. In the other type of hearing aid, amplifier vibrations are carried directly to the bones of the skull. This is done by an attachment that fits against the bone behind the ear.

Some people get discouraged when they first try a hearing aid. They find it hard to pick out the conversations they want from all the other magnified sounds the microphone picks up. But with patience and training, most are able to adjust to hearing aids, just as the visually impaired are able to adjust to wearing glasses.

In neural or central hearing loss, the sound is conducted to the inner ear, but there is a defect in the auditory nerve that carries the impulse to the brain. Something prevents the proper electrical signals from being transmitted and received.

Neural and central hearing loss occurs at the beginning and toward the end of life. It is associated with the very young and the very old. Damage or defects occur as a result of blood incompatibility between mother and child, rubella during pregnancy, or shortage of oxygen at the time of delivery. Or, it occurs as part of the aging process and degenerative changes in the later years.

Doctors cannot usually correct neural or central hearing loss. Most youngsters with this disability require hearing aids, and special education and training.

New techniques now used in hospitals lessen the effects of blood incompatibility. Improved methods in the delivery room also ensure a proper supply of oxygen to babies before and after birth. Vaccines are available to protect pregnant women against a number of viruses, including rubella. And new tests are being used to locate nerve damage in very young children.

Many who are born deaf are mistakenly believed to be born "dumb," that is, mute, and not able to speak. While there are some few people with a hearing disorder who also have disorders which prevent speech, almost all deaf persons are able to speak. Often, they do not speak because they lack sufficient hearing to understand speech. Never having understood the sounds of speech, they find it hard to produce these sounds accurately.

Some educators believe in hand or manual communication for people with severe hearing loss. These methods depend on sign language and finger spelling. It is easier for people with a severe hearing disability to learn sign language than to learn to speak.

Others find the manual method too limited. It restricts communication to others who are deaf, since few hearing people learn sign language. Children who are only taught manual communication become cut off from spoken language. Persons who become deaf after having acquired speech lose the language skills that they once had. Since the language of signs does not follow the structure of the English language, using it exclusively can cause reading and writing difficulties.

The oral method, which helps children to speak as well as they can and uses lip-reading or speech-reading to understand others, also has some problems. Some young children, not familiar with the sounds of speech, take a very long time to learn oral speech. By the time they master it, many years of valuable educational and communication experiences may have been lost.

Many educators now favor the total communication approach. This combination of hand and oral language lets individuals use the method that works best for them. They believe that total communication deals better with the wide range of differences found among children with hearing disabilities.

The disagreement over methods of teaching children with serious hearing problems is as nothing compared to the current controversy over the best setting for their education. Should children who are deaf be educated in regular public schools or in special schools for the deaf?

Those who favor mainstreaming youngsters in regular classrooms argue that since deaf youngsters live in a hearing world, they should attend school with hearing youngsters. Also, they hold that the wider range of experiences will not only help to develop these children educationally, but socially and emotionally as well. Education in special schools may mean taking children out of their communities and away from their peers. Isolation can lead to dependency and eccentricity.

The position against mainstreaming is that most regular classroom teachers are not qualified or experienced in educating youngsters who are deaf. They need to adapt their methods to the special needs of these youngsters. Otherwise, the deaf children become lost in the shuffle.

The deaf child who is speech-reading cannot follow a teacher who talks and writes on the board at the same time; or one who makes comments while showing films in a room where it is too dark to see signs or speech-read. The child who is not able to hear is often ignored and left out of many conversations and activities. While most agree that children with slight hearing losses can be successfully integrated, they fear that the experiences for the more severely disabled would be poor.

The deaf child who grows up in a home with hearing parents usually has many additional problems. Communication between the hearing and the deaf is often difficult. Where there is little communication, children may not learn the most ordinary life skills—dressing, personal hygiene, shopping, money, sex information, and so on. Sometimes the children go for several years without either oral language or the ability to use sign language. They are retarded in social and academic development. When they go to school, they are far behind the others. Deaf children of deaf parents usually are able to communicate more easily with their parents, and hence may avoid many of these problems.

Persons who grow up with profound hearing loss and poor educational or social development may not have confidence in their ability to function well in social and business situations. Often they are unsure of themselves, apprehensive, and resentful. Recent studies of deaf students in regular colleges and universities showed that these students preferred to spend their free time with other deaf students.

Some people with mild hearing loss try to hide their disability. They strain to listen to speech too soft for them to hear comfortably, and have to guess at the words they miss. This can be very tiring, and may lead to nervousness and irritability. Avoiding contacts with the hearing is one way that they deal with the fear of not being able to hear what is being said.

Not only do deaf people face problems in day-to-day living, but there are special difficulties too. It is often hard for deaf people to give information to the police, because their speech may be difficult to understand.

Recently, a thirteen-year-old deaf boy was playing in a vacant building. The owner of the building ordered him to leave, but the boy did not hear him. In a fit of anger, the man shot and killed the boy. Later, when told that the boy was deaf, the man confessed that that possibility had never occurred to him.

Some progress is being made in caring for the special needs of deaf people — in education, in social contacts, in day-to-day activities, and in the world of work. The new laws and the debates on mainstreaming are leading to improved ways of educating children with hearing loss.

People who do not have hearing difficulties need to become more comfortable with those who do. They need to learn to look straight at the person and to speak slowly. Television needs to program more events in sign language, so the millions in our society who cannot hear can have the experience of enjoying newscasts, sports, dramas, and other programs. More trains and buses have to be equipped with warning lights to alert non-hearing people to danger.

D. L. Colton of Minneapolis, Minnesota, who is deaf, is working on a new self-help approach. He has trained a "hearing" dog to help him in much the same way a seeing-eye dog helps the blind. At the sound of an alarm clock, a smoke alarm, or a knock on the door the dog is trained to nudge its owner, run to the source of the sound, and then back to the owner.

Self-help, social awareness, new laws, and more opportunities for integration into society are important ways to bring the deaf and the hearing segments of the population closer together.

MULTIPLE HANDICAPS

The increase in the number of people in our society who have more than one handicap is, oddly enough, related to recent advances in medicine.

In the past, children who were born with serious birth defects did not survive. They died at an early age. But with the discovery of new drugs, new treatments, and new surgical methods, doctors are able to save and prolong the lives of these infants. Consequently, many more persons born with serious impairments are reaching maturity.

Rubella, or German measles, is generally a rather mild disease. But when it attacks a mother during the first three months of pregnancy, the effects on the unborn child can be very damaging. These children are frequently born blind, deaf, mentally retarded, and with impairments of the heart and nervous system. In 1964 and 1965, a widespread rubella epidemic swept the United States. Thousands of babies affected by rubella before birth were born impaired. Many showed the multiple handicaps that are sometimes called the "rubella syndrome." Some people who are deaf and blind are victims of rubella.

Another important cause of multiple handicaps

is an inherited condition known as Usher's syndrome. The affected infants are born deaf. Then, at age seven or eight, they begin to lose their sight. The loss is actually a narrowing of the visual field, like looking through progressively narrowing tubes, until the child can see only a pinpoint of light. Then even that disappears, and the child is entirely without vision.

Multiple handicaps also occur as a result of other disabilities. Cerebral palsy, for example, is often accompanied by hearing loss and farsightedness. Muscular dystrophy and diseases of the central nervous system are frequently associated with degeneration of the retina of the eye. Children with multiple sclerosis sometimes suffer damage to the optic nerve. Juvenile diabetes mellitus can lead to cataracts.

Estimates on the numbers of multiply handicapped vary from 12,000 to 20,000. Exact numbers are not known. Most are deaf and blind. Although they share some problems with people who are "only" blind or "only" deaf, they do have distinct needs of their own.

Unable to use the most important sense organ, the eyes, or the second most important sense, hearing, those who are blind-deaf usually learn a one-hand manual alphabet that is sometimes referred to as finger spelling. The teacher forms the finger positions within the trainee's cupped hands and teaches the meaning of the word by associating it with something the youngster can touch. It is a long, hard process that requires lots of patience on the part of the teacher and the student.

Then, deaf-blind people may be taught to hear by placing their fingers lightly on the mouth and throat of the speaker. If they are very determined, they can learn to speak and express their thoughts orally. But in talking to others who are multiply handicapped, they form the symbols of the manual alphabet into the listener's hand.

Instruction in braille is part of the education of every deaf-blind person. First, it opens up writing as another channel of communication. And second, it enables them, since they cannot listen to the radio, records, or tapes, or to watch television, to be able to read.

Not long ago, thirty deaf and blind people from as many nations met in New York City for the first major international conference on problems of the multiply handicapped. One of the delegates was Sergei Sirotkin. Mr. Sirotkin is a twenty-eight-year-old Russian who recently became one of four deaf-blind people in the Soviet Union to graduate from a university. Sergei began his special training when he was only five years old.

This group needs more specialized institutions tailored to their particular needs. The Helen Keller National Center for Deaf-Blind Youth and Adults in Sands Point, New York, is the first such institution set up for the training and rehabilitation of persons who can neither see nor hear.

The school is not too different from other buildings in its physical aspects. But it is safer and more convenient. It incorporates many solutions to the daily problems of the multiply handicapped.

At the Center, the individual's alarm clock, for example, is connected to a vibrator that is attached to the bedsprings. When the alarm sounds, the bed vibrates until the person shuts the alarm off. When you push a doorbell, the button turns on a fan. The surge of air alerts the resident that someone is at the door. Push buttons both inside and outside the elevators are labeled in braille. Passengers can keep their fingers on floor-indicator buttons that pop out as the car passes each floor.

The end of carpeting on the floor signals the beginning of steps. There are handrails along the steps. The end of the rail indicates the end of the steps.

Since lack of exercise is a problem of the deaf-blind, the Center has an outdoor roller skating rink and a jogging track. Waist-high rails serve as guides around the track. The gym is equipped for workouts to help release tensions, as well as to build up strength and stamina. Here the floor slopes upward at the edge to warn the users of the approach of a wall.

The sidewalks and streets around the Center's buildings are paved with gravel, bricks, or dirt. The students learn how to travel independently. They learn to go over an obstacle course that is bumpy and curved, with a large rock in the middle. They even have a sidewalk with a driveway to accustom people to avoiding moving or parked cars. Once trainees can get around these courses, they are taught to make their way on public streets and on public vehicles.

Trainees learn to do cooking, cleaning, and other household chores in the Center's model apartment. Appliances have braille strips on them. The heat regulator on the oven is notched like a clock; a notch in the 6 o'clock position means medium heat; 9 o'clock signifies high heat.

Deaf-blind students also learn factory operations. One young man was taught to operate a power saw. When he returns home, he will take a job in a plant where sheets of aluminum are cut up into strips. Other trainees will become assemblers on factory production lines, work in sheltered workshops, or find some other employment.

The hope for the deaf-blind who reach for life and happiness is summed up best by one of the officials at the Helen Keller Center, who is himself blind and deaf:

> I call it life,
> And laugh with delight,
> Though life itself is
> Out of sound and sight.

10 A NEW DAY

We have come a long way since primitive times when persons with disabilities were put to death or cast from their families. We have improved the care and treatment of disabled persons. We have moved from doling out pity and charity to the disabled to finding ways to meet their basic need for work and independence. At a time when there are laws to protect the civil liberties of individuals regardless of age, sex, class, and racial or ethnic background, we are making progress in guaranteeing and protecting the liberties of disabled persons.

The federal Education of All Handicapped Children Act, Public Law 94–142, is, we have said, sometimes called the Bill of Rights for the Handicapped. The law sets up specific requirements for the education of the eight million handicapped children in our country. Under the broad definition of the law, the handicapped include those who are "mentally retarded, hard of hearing, deaf, speech impaired, visually handicapped, severely emotionally disturbed, orthopedically handicapped or other health impaired children or children with specific learning disabilities." The main purpose of the law is to correct the educational practices that have deprived many of these children of a sound education.

Basically, P. L. 94–142 requires that states and local school districts locate all school-aged children with handicaps and provide for them a free and appropriate education. Each handicapped child is to have an Individual Education Plan (I.E.P.) worked out by school officials, the child's teacher, his or her parents or guardians, and — if possible — by the child as well. A review of each child's I.E.P. is to be carried out yearly. And the handicapped child is to be educated in classes with non-handicapped children to the greatest extent possible.

Mainstreaming offers many benefits to both the disabled and the able-bodied.

Placing handicapped youngsters in regular classes is called mainstreaming. The chief goals of mainstreaming are to provide a better learning environment for handicapped children, to improve their social status, and to provide experiences in school that more closely resemble life outside the classroom.

Many now consider special classes for the handicapped a form of segregation. Recent studies show that for the most part handicapped students do better in regular classes than in special classes. Educators have also learned that labeling children and placing them in special classes can have a negative effect on them as students.

The benefits of P. L. 94–142 extend far beyond the 10 to 12 percent of the school population who are handicapped. Its advantages reach all students. When handicapped and non-handicapped are brought together, all students learn to cooperate and understand one another. Mike, "the deaf boy," becomes better known as Mike, "the track star," or Mike, "the kid who is a whiz at math." Mike's friends know that he has his share of strong and weak points, just as they do. And Mike learns how to get along with hearing adults and peers.

The great hope is that mainstreaming will become more than a practice followed in school. Mainstreaming needs to become a way of life. Handicapped and non-handicapped should be brought together in all aspects of community activity — in recreation programs, religious services, scouting, civic and political groups, as well as in offices, stores, and factories.

P. L. 94–142 works closely with Section 504 of the Rehabilitation Act (P. L. 93–112). P. L. 93–112 is a general law that forbids discrimination against handicapped individuals in education or employment. This means, in some cases, the removal of architectural barriers in schools and public buildings. Ramps and elevators are being installed, doorways are being widened, and other structural changes are being made.

These changes, too, do not only benefit the disabled. They make it easier for toddlers and the elderly to get around safely. They help people who are pushing baby carriages or strollers, using shopping carts, riding bicycles, and so on.

A story is told about two towns in which there was plenty of food but the people were not able to feed themselves because they could not bend their arms at the elbows. In one town, the people starved and died. But in the other town the people were well-fed. The reason for the difference was that the people in the second town were feeding each other. In a society where people share and show compassion to one another, human disabilities become very unimportant.

BIBLIOGRAPHY

Bleck, Eugene E., and Nagel, Donald A. *Physically Handicapped Children: A Medical Atlas for Teachers.* New York: Grune and Stratton, 1975.

Boynick, David K. *Champions by Setback: Athletes Who Overcame Physical Handicaps.* New York: Thomas Y. Crowell, 1954.

Connor, Frances P. *Education of Exceptional Children and Youth.* Englewood Cliffs: Prentice-Hall, 1975.

Cruikshank, W. M. *Psychology of Exceptional Children and Youth.* Englewood Cliffs: Prentice-Hall, 1971.

Hallhan and Kauffman. *Exceptional Children: An Introduction to Special Education.* Englewood Cliffs: Prentice-Hall, 1978.

Massie, Robert and Suzanne. *Journey.* New York: Alfred A. Knopf, 1973.

Rusk, Howard. *A World To Care For.* New York: Random House, 1972.

Spock, Benjamin, and Lerrigo, Marion. *Caring For Your Disabled Child.* New York: Macmillan, 1965.

SOURCES OF STATISTICS

The Killers and Cripplers: Facts on the Major Diseases in the U.S. Today. Compiled by The National Health Education Committee. David McKay, 1976.

One in Eleven: Handicapped Adults in America. President's Committee on Employment of the Handicapped, December 1974.

FURTHER READING

Cavanah, Frances. *Triumphant Adventure: The Story of Franklin Delano Roosevelt.* Chicago: Rand McNally, 1964. A great leader triumphs over polio.

Charlip, Remy. *Handtalk, an ABC of Finger Spelling and Sign Language.* New York: Parent's Magazine Press, 1974. A book that can teach you how to communicate without oral speech.

Fassler, Joan. *Howie Helps Himself.* Chicago: Albert Whitman and Co., 1975. Realistic story of a young boy in a wheelchair.

Hasegawa, Sam. *Stevie Wonder.* Mankato, Minn.: Creative Education, 1975. Popular blind music star wins the adulation of millions.

Keller, Helen. *The Story of My Life.* Garden City: Doubleday, 1954. Autobiography of the woman who overcame blindness and deafness.

Savitz, Harriet May. *On the Move.* New York: John Day and Co., 1973. A girl with paraplegia learns that she can lead an independent life.

Southall, Ivan. *Let the Balloon Go.* New York: St. Martin's Press, 1968. A tale about a boy with cerebral palsy who learns to do things for himself.

Stein, Sarah Bonnett. *About Handicaps.* New York: Walker and Co., 1974. Story of a boy and his friend who has cerebral palsy.

Sullivan, Tom, and Gill, Derek. *If You Could See What I Hear.* New York: Harper and Row, 1975. Autobiography of Tom, blind from birth, who develops his abilities as a singer, athlete, student, husband, and father.

Valens, E. G. *A Long Way Up, the Story of Jill Kinmont.* New York: Harper and Row, 1966. A fine athlete tells of her life after her spinal cord was severed in a skiing accident.

Viscardi, Henry. *A Man's Stature.* New York: John Day and Co., 1952. Fascinating autobiography of a leading figure in the education and training of people with severe physical disabilities who was himself born without legs.

Wolf, Bernard. *Don't Feel Sorry for Paul.* Philadelphia and New York: J. B. Lippincott Co., 1974. Two weeks in the life of Paul, who has a lot of excitement despite a disabling physical condition.

PUBLICATIONS AVAILABLE
FROM THE FOLLOWING:

American Speech and Hearing Association, 919 Eighteenth Street, N.W., Washington, D.C. 20006

Arthritis Foundation, 1212 Avenue of the Americas, New York, N.Y. 10036

Bureau of Education for the Handicapped, U.S. Office of Education, Seventh and D Streets, S.W., Washington, D.C. 20202

Center for the Multiple Handicapped, 105 East 106 Street, New York, N.Y. 10029

Epilepsy Foundation of America, 1828 L Street, N.W., Suite 406, Washington, D.C. 20036

Muscular Dystrophy Association of America, 810 Seventh Ave., New York, N.Y. 10019

National Amputation Foundation, 12–45 150 Street, Whitestone, New York 11357

National Cystic Fibrosis Foundation, 521 Fifth Avenue, New York, N.Y. 10017

National Hemophilia Foundation, 25 West 39 Street, New York, N.Y. 10018

National Multiple Sclerosis Society, 257 Park Avenue South, New York, N.Y. 10010

Office for the Blind and Visually Handicapped, Department of Health, Education, and Welfare, 330 C Street, S.W., Washington, D.C. 20201

President's Committee on Employment of the Handicapped, Washington, D.C. 20210

Spina Bifida Association of America, 343 South Dearborn Avenue, Suite 319, Chicago, Illinois 60604

INDEX

Abilities, Inc., 62
Alexander the Great, 44
Allergens, 81–83
Allergy, 81
American Blind Bowling Association, 95
Amputation, 7, 11, 12, 17, 18, 61–64
Anemia, 69, 83–85
    sickle cell, 83–84
Arthritis, 65, 72
    juvenile rheumatoid arthritis (JRA), 65–67
Artificial limbs, 28, 62, 63
Asthma, 69, 81–83
Astigmatism, 90
Ataxia. See Cerebral palsy
Athetosis. See Cerebral palsy

Barden-LaFollette Act, 21
Barriers, 3, 5, 29, 112
Beethoven, Ludwig van, 10
Blind, 3, 10, 11, 12, 18, 31, 78, 87, 88–96, 103
Blind-deaf, 103, 104, 105
Blind Golfers tournaments, 89, 95

Blue babies, 75
Bone and joint disorders, 61–67
Boswell, Charlie, 88–89, 95
Braces, 55, 57, 71
Braille, 88, 92–94, 105, 106
Braille, Louis, 94
Braillewriter, 94
Brain injury, 35–36, 41, 42
Bridgman, Laura, 18
Bronchitis, 79

Caesar, Julius, 44
Calvin, John, 16
Calvinism, 16
Cancer, 63
Cataract, 91, 104
Central nervous system, 34, 46, 55, 57, 104
Cerebral palsy, 9, 17, 27, 34–40, 52, 90, 104
    ataxia, 38
    athetosis, 36, 38
    mixed, 38
    rigidity, 38
    spasticity, 36, 38,
    tremor, 38

Chronic health problems, 69–85
Clubfoot, 53
Cogswell, Alice, 18
Convulsions. See Seizures
Counselors, 28
Cross-eyes, 90
Crutches, 55, 57
Cryosurgery, 39
Cunningham, Glenn, 11
Cyanosis, 75
Cystic fibrosis, 69, 79–81

Deaf, 3, 10, 11, 12, 18, 87, 96–103
Deaf-blind. See Blind-deaf
Diabetes, 69, 77–79
    juvenile diabetes mellitus, 91, 104
Disabilities. See Physical disabilities
Dorsch, George, 62
Dostoyevsky, Fyodor Mikhailovich, 44
Down's syndrome. See Mental retardation
Duchenne-type. See Muscular dystrophy

Education of All Handicapped Children Act, See Public Law 94–142
Elementary and Secondary Education Act, 22
Epilepsy, 40–44
    grand mal, 42
    petit mal, 42, 43
    psychomotor, 43
Eye, 89–90

Facia-scapulo-humeral type, See Muscular dystrophy

Farsightedness, 90, 104
Finger spelling, 99, 104

Gallaudet, Thomas Hopkins, 18
Gallaudet College, 18
German measles. See Rubella
Glaucoma, 91
Grand mal. See Epilepsy
Guttman, Dr. Ludwig, 58–59

Handel, George Frederic, 44
Handicaps. See Physical handicaps
Hartford (Conn.) School for the Deaf, 18
Hearing aid, 98, 99
Hearing loss, 97, 98, 104
Heart disease, 12, 69, 73–76, 78, 81, 103
Heine, Heinrich, 10
Helen Keller Center, 105–107
Hemophilia, 69–73
Homer, 10
Hopkins, Stephen, 17, 38
Howe, Samuel Gridley, 18
Human Resources School, 62–63
Humpback, 53
Hydrocephalus, 54
Hyperopia. See Farsightedness

Idiopathic scoliosis. See Scoliosis.
Individual Education Plan (I.E.P), 109
Injection, 77–78, 79, 82

Juvenile diabetes mellitus. See Diabetes
Juvenile rheumatoid arthritis. See Arthritis

Keller, Helen, 11, 18, 95
Kyphosis. *See* Humpback

Limb-girdle form. *See* Muscular dystrophy
Lip-reading, 100
Lordosis. *See* Swayback
Lung disease, 81

Mainstreaming, 100–102, 111–112
Manual communication, 99
March epilepsy. *See* Epilepsy, psychomotor
Massie, Bobby, 71, 85
May, Morris, 17
Meningocele. *See* Spina bifada
Mental retardation, 54, 91, 103
Milton, John, 10
Milwaukee Brace, 64–65
Mixed cerebral palsy. *See* Cerebral palsy
Multiple handicaps, 103–107
Multiple sclerosis, 46–47, 57, 104
Muscular dystrophy, 7, 47–52, 57, 104
  duchenne type, 50–51
  facio-scapula-humeral type, 51
  limb-girdle form, 51
Myelomeningocele. *See* Spina bifada
Myopia. *See* Nearsightedness

National Wheelchair Games, 59
Nearsightedness, 90
Nerve and muscle disorders, 7, 11, 34–44

Open-heart surgery, 75

Optacon, 94
Oral method, 100

Pacemakers, 39
Paralympics. *See* Wheelchair sports
Paralysis, 10, 11, 12, 13, 35, 53, 54, 57–59
Paraplegia, 57–59
Parents, 27, 28, 29, 51, 55, 69, 91, 92, 101
Pasteur, Louis, 11
Perkins Institute, 18
Perlman, Itzhak, 11
Petit mal. *See* Epilepsy
Physical disabilities
  causes, 7–9, 13, 16
  definition, 7–13
  history, 5–23
    ancient, 15, 109
    colonial America, 17
    Greeks, 15–16
    Hebrews, 15
    Middle Ages, 16
    Nineteenth century, 18–19
    Renaissance, 16
    Revolutionary War, 17
    Romans, 15
    Twentieth century, 20
    World War I, 20–21
    World War II, 21
  identification, 7
  statistics, 9
Physical therapy, 39, 50, 57, 63, 64, 66
Pneumonia, 79
Polio, 10, 11, 55–59
Polio vaccine, 56
Poliomyelitis. *See* Polio
Prostheses. *See* Artificial limbs
Protestant idea, 18

Psychological problems, 25–32, 63, 67, 72–73, 76, 81, 101–102
Psychomotor. *See* Epilepsy
Public Law, 16, 21
Public Law 93–112, 23, 111–112
Public Law 94–142, 22–23, 109–112

Quadriplegia, 57

Rehabilitation Act. *See* Public Law 93–112
Respiratory disease, 49, 97
Rheumatic fever, 76
Rheumatism, 65
Rigidity. *See* Cerebral palsy
Rockerbottom foot, 53
Roosevelt, Franklin Delano, 10, 57
Rubella, 98, 103
Rudolph, Wilma, 11

Scoliosis, 49, 53, 64–65
Seizures, 39, 40, 41, 42, 44
Seversky, Alexander de, 11
Sheltered workshops, 29
Shunt, 54, 55
Siblings, 27, 28, 51, 69, 92
Sickle cell anemia. *See* Anemia
Sign language 18, 99, 101, 102
Sirotkin, Sergei, 105
Smith Sears Vocational Rehabilitation Act, 20–21
Snellen chart, 90
Spasticity. *See* Cerebral palsy
Speech reading, 100

Spina bifada, 52–55, 57
  meningocele, 52–53
  myelomeningocele, 53–54
  occulta, 52, 53
Steinmetz, Charles, 10
Stevens, Thaddeus, 20
Stoke Mandeville Hospital, 58
Strabismus. *See* Crosseyes
Stroke, 78
Stuyvesant, Peter, 17
Surgery, 54, 62, 90, 97
Swayback, 53
Sweat test, 79

Tchaikowsky, Peter Ilich, 44
Title IV, 22
Total communication, 100
Tremor. *See* Cerebral palsy
Trudeau, Edward Livingston, 20
Tuberculosis, 20

Unemployment, 29
Ushers syndrome, 104

Van Gogh, Vincent, 44
Viscardi, Henry "Hank," 61–63
Visual impairment. *See* Blind
Vocational Rehabilitation Act, 21

Wheelchair sports, 58, 59, 62
Wheelchairs, 28
Wittgenstein, Paul, 11
Workmen's compensation, 20

Yanover, Dr. Robert, 62